THE CHILI COOKBOOK

By Johnrae Earl and James McCormick

PRICE/STERN/SLOAN
Publishers, Inc., Los Angeles

THIRD PRINTING — JULY 1973

Copyright © 1972 by Johnrae Earl and James McCormick
Published by Price/Stern/Sloan Publishers, Inc.
410 North La Cienega Boulevard, Los Angeles, California 90048
Printed in the United States of America. All rights reserved.
Library of Congress Catalog Card Number: 72-81740
ISBN: 0-8431-0186-5

SOME LORE BEFORE 11

DALLAS COUNTY JAILHOUSE CHILI 17
AMARILLO 18
HOUSTON'S BEST 19
SAN ANTONIO 20

INGREDIENTS 21

BASIC CHILIS 25

MASA MASA 28
LADY BIRD JOHNSON'S PEDERNALES RIVER SPECIAL 29
PANCHO VILLA 30
SWEET SUET 31
IT'S THE DICKENS 32
A BIT OF MEXICO 33
THICK AND SASSY 34
JALAPEÑO AUTHENTICO 35
STOMACH WARMER 36
RAPIDO 37
HOT PANTS STYLE 38
SHADES OF TEXAS 39
THE BROWN DERBY 40
DEEP BREATHER 41
KID'S DELIGHT 42
DAD'S FAVORITE 43

LET IT STAND **44**
BLANCO'S RIO GRANDE **45**
A BED OF BEANS **46**

PINTO BEAN CHILIS **47**

BASIC PINTO BEANS **49**
ONIONS AND STUFF **50**
CHASEN'S FAMOUS CHILI **51**
CANNONADEER **52**
OLD CARNEY **53**
THE SLY ONE **54**
SLIGHTLY SMASHED **55**
EVEN STEPHEN **56**
THREE-HOUR BEANS **57**
TOGETHERNESS **58**
VEGETARIAN DREAMBOAT **59**
TAPS **60**

KIDNEY BEAN CHILIS **61**

ACCENT ON PEPPERCORNS **64**
MIDWEST CAYENNE **65**
MUSHROOM SNIFFLE **66**
TEAR-JERKER **67**
FOR MILLIONAIRES ONLY **68**
FAR WEST **69**

THE S.S. JOHNNIE   **70**

IT'S PICKLED   **71**

PORKY   **72**

ADVENTURING   **73**

GREEN PEPPER   **74**

WATERFRONT   **75**

COMMUNAL   **76**

MINNESOTA STYLE   **77**

BREATHE EASY   **78**

HOT CHILIS   **79**

FIRE CALL   **84**

NO EXIT   **85**

SCORCHER   **86**

VOLCANO   **87**

HOT PORKER   **88**

HELL'S FIRE   **89**

NO RETREAT   **90**

WHEN AUTUMN COMES   **91**

INFERNO   **92**

CHUNKY CHILIS   **93**

SIRLOIN AND RICE   **96**

ALLEGHENY HIGHWAY   **97**

NO TOMATOES, PLEASE!   **98**

CINNAMON FLAVORED **99**

BOUILLON AND MUSHROOMS **100**

OFF THE FARM **101**

ON THE PATIO **102**

COCOA FLAVORED **103**

AZTECA **104**

TRUCK STOP **105**

WHEELER-DEALER **106**

IOWA RED **107**

A LA SPAGHETTI **108**

BY ANY OTHER NAME **109**

DASH OF CURRY **110**

CONVENIENCE CHILIS 111

NO STRAIN **113**

EASY DOES IT **114**

SPONTANEOUS **115**

FEW RULES **116**

LEISURE TIME **117**

RING-AROUND **118**

DEXTEROUS **119**

NO EFFORT **120**

HEAT IT UP **121**

HOME LATE **122**

STANDBY **123**

ON THE RUN **124**

PRESTO! **125**

HURRY UP! **126**

ODD FELLOW CHILIS **127**

LIVERPOOL **130**

NAPLES **131**

ATHENS **132**

EL GHERIAT ESC-SCHERGHIA **133**

VALENCIA **134**

BOGOTÁ **135**

TORONTO **136**

MIAMI BEACH **137**

KUALA LUMPUR **138**

NEW DELHI **139**

BUENOS AIRES **140**

TEL AVIV **141**

BERLIN **142**

GUADALAJARA **143**

COPENHAGEN **144**

NAGASAKI **145**

KATMANDU **146**

HEIDELBERG **147**

CAPE TOWN **148**

INDEX 149

Being the first complete collection of Chili Con Carne recipes ever assembled . . . including sectional variations and eccentricities in preparing the famous dish throughout the United States, and a special chapter on authentic chilis from all over the world.

SOME LORE BEFORE

The Chili Cookbook provides more ways to make Chili Con Carne (red peppers, meat and sometimes beans) than anybody ever dreamed existed. It also contributes in a small way to one of the great debates of modern times — The Great Chili Controversy.

Where did the dish originate? Is the addition of tomatoes and onions, and various beans such as red, kidney and pinto, an evolutionary step or an adulteration? What about thick versus thin? How many spices and which ones? How classic is the inclusion of maize?

In addition to exploring these questions, *The Chili Cookbook* offers one hundred recipes for Chili Con Carne grouped into seven classifications: "Basic," "Pinto Bean," "Kidney Bean," "Hot," "Chunky," "Convenience" and "Odd Fellow," gathered from around the world and modified slightly for adaptation in the modern American kitchen. All have been selected from more than six hundred recipes collected and tested by the editors themselves.

A Bit of Blasphemy

The editors have never believed that the inventive and tasty dish known around the world as Chili Con Carne was originated by the braggarts of Texas, as Frank X. Tolbert, author of *A Bowl of Red*, and the Texas chili consortium (The International Chili Appreciation Society of Dallas) would have us believe. If it had, the tasteless and vapid product known as Texas style chili would never have gotten off the ground.

12

Quoting from letters and records and tall stories told by older Texans, the best Tolbert can do is place the first mention of Chili Con Carne in Texas around 1824, when cattle range cooks, an ornery breed of lazy cowpunchers who had grown too stiff-jointed to mount a horse, began adapting from the poorer classes of San Antonio (comprised chiefly of Mexicans) a dish in which the meat was "generally cut into a kind of hash with nearly as many peppers as there are pieces of meat — all this is stewed together."

Yet history records that meat, beans, peppers and herbs were mixed with maize by the highly sophisticated Inca, Aztec and Mayan Indians long before the arrival of Columbus or the Spanish Conquistadores. Then the Spanish modified this to their liking, and further changes were made by various South American and Central American Indians. The little red, yellow or purplish pod from the woody plant of the nightshade family, variously called the Guinea pepper, the Spanish pepper or the chili pepper, also was well-known in England through the latter half of the sixteenth century when English ships carried it to London from the Netherlands East Indies. Even earlier than that the pepper was in common use as a condiment throughout Spain, and one of Miguel de Cervantes' favorite dishes during his wacky La Mancha period was a soup prepared by his wife, Catalina, made from a dog bone, water and pepper pods, brought to a boil and simmered for two days.

Obviously then, God in his spatial overview didn't leave it up to Texans to be the first people on earth to mix the red pepper with meat and serve it in a bowl.

It's also useful to know that "the original bowl of Texas chili" on which Tolbert and the 209-member consortium base their claim, uses no tomatoes. The scrivener Tolbert says: "The emphasis in this book *(A Bowl of Red)* will be on the world-famous, seldom-found-today, original, Texas-style bowl of red. I happen to be a fourth generation Texan and so open to charges of chauvinism when I say that the best chili is now made in Texas, and has been made in this province since the *dim beginnings of this piperine delight.*" (A version of this dubious taste treat will be found in the recipe in this book under the title "Shades of Texas".)

As a matter of fact, the tomato originated in Peru, Ecuador and Bolivia and was cultivated and eaten — and always in chili dishes — for centuries before Columbus. North of the Rio Grande, however, a wild species of tomato was known but was considered inedible, even poisonous, by the Caucasians who lived there. This probably explains why the Johnnies-come-lately from Texas call Chili Con Carne without tomatoes "the best chili."

In real life, that stricture against tomatoes, and another, that beans, if desired, are cooked separately and added to the chili last, and another, that kidney beans are never to be used, all are themselves filled with the wind of the bean. It's a fact that chili is popular in Texas. But most of the recipes relished there *DO* contain tomatoes and *DO* contain beans cooked right in the same old pot, and many *DO* use kidney beans.

The chili that's named for Amarillo, for instance, uses tomatoes, tomato paste and kidney beans all cooked together. Houston's best chili tosses in kidney beans, tomatoes *AND* tomato juice. And Charlie's Famous Chili from Waco is anything but Tolbert's dream. It contains tomato paste, kidney beans, tomatoes, Worcestershire sauce and, of all things, beef gravy!

Mrs. Lyndon B. Johnson's recipe (it will be found elsewhere in this book) uses tomatoes, too. But it is a terrible Chili Con Carne. Among true chili lovers it is known as "sloppy" because of the careless amount of water used in it.

The only so-called true Texas chili the editors have been able to find that is worth the salt put into it, is the famous Dallas County Jailhouse Chili. This is made the way Tolbert and the consortium would want it to be made, but even this permits the addition of beans, if desired.

As for the other ingredients in Chili Con Carne — herbs and a multitude of spices — most of them have been known since time began. The red pepper itself, having originated in Eastern Malaysia, is an oriental pepper and is not from South America as is generally believed. And only the Malaysians, the Chinese, Mexicans, Italians and the Spanish know how to release its full power. In rural Mexico, for example, the whole peppers are ground in a granite bowl with a granite ball grinder, and with the addition of one or two tomatoes all the rich, tasty oils of the chili pods are brought forth. At home in modern Mexico City, though, they say a kitchen blender does almost as well.

In all fairness, there is little that can be said for the association of Texas with Chili Con Carne, except that loud talk and an ignorance of the world at large allow them to perpetuate the myth that they created the dish. They have even adopted the name "Chili Parlor" as theirs, when in fact it was used around Titusville, Pennsylvania, when Edwin Drake sank America's first oil well and started a boom that led to the brand name Freedom-Valvoline. "Parlor" was a fitting name for a chili joint at that time; it was an old English term for a dining room in an inn or tavern fitted for conversation.

About all Texans have really done for chili is alter its name from Nahuatl "chilli" to "chili" and spread that misspelling around the world. But that is a matter that chili lovers in Springfield, Illinois, are trying to correct with a mushrooming of places calling themselves "Chilli Joints."

Following are four of the very best chili recipes the editors have found that Texas has to offer. The reader is invited to try them all before turning to the more imaginative recipes to be found later in these pages.

DALLAS COUNTY
(Serves 6 to 8) JAILHOUSE CHILI

¼ pound beef suet
2 pounds coarse ground beef (aged beef, if possible)
3 cups water
3 cloves garlic, chopped
3 tablespoons paprika
3 teaspoons chili powder
1 teaspoon ground cumin
1 teaspoon salt
1 teaspoon white pepper
1½ teaspoons sweet peppers, diced

Melt suet in pot. Add meat and simmer, covered, for four hours, stirring frequently. Add water a little at a time. Add all other ingredients and simmer one more hour. If you insist on beans, add one can of your favorite, drained, before serving.

AMARILLO *(Serves 6)*

2 pounds ground chuck
1 can (1½ oz.) chili powder
2 teaspoons salt
½ teaspoon pepper
¼ teaspoon sugar
3 cloves garlic, chopped fine
2 large onions, chopped fine
1 can (16 oz.) tomatoes, broken up
3 cans (6 oz.) tomato paste
6 tomato paste cans water
3 cans (20 oz.) dark kidney beans, drained

Sauté ground chuck and chili powder, being careful not to scorch powder. Add salt, pepper, sugar, garlic and onions. Cook together until onion is translucent (about five minutes). Add tomatoes, tomato paste and water. Simmer, covered, for one-and-one-half hours. Add beans, heat through and serve.

HOUSTON'S BEST

1 pound dried red kidney beans
1 medium red onion, cut in half
salt and pepper to taste
1½ pounds ground chuck
1 large Bermuda onion, chopped
½ cup green pepper, chopped
1 pound chopped round steak

½ teaspoon paprika
3 tablespoons chili powder
pinch crushed red pepper
1 package chili mix
1 can (8 oz.) stewed tomatoes
1 can (8 oz.) tomato juice
1 teaspoon flour, dissolved
in ½ cup cold water

Soak beans overnight with red onion, salt and pepper to taste. Five hours before serving time, sauté ground chuck together with chopped onion, green pepper and chopped round steak. Stir in all other ingredients except beans and flour-water mixture. Simmer, covered, for three hours. Thicken by stirring in flour-water mixture and cooking a bit more. Combine beans and chili and serve hot.

SAN ANTONIO *(Serves 6)*

1 pound dry kidney beans, soaked overnight
1 large onion
2 pounds ground beef
3 cloves garlic, minced
2 small onions, chopped fine
½ cup rendered chicken fat
3 tablespoons chili powder
salt to taste
1 can (8 oz.) tomato soup

Cook beans and the large onion with water to cover until beans are tender (about one hour). Remove onion and set beans aside. Brown meat with the small chopped onions and the garlic in chicken fat. Stir in chili powder and salt and stir meat often while browning. When meat is brown, add it to the beans and the water in which they were cooked. Add tomato soup and simmer fifteen minutes, stirring often to keep from scorching.

INGREDIENTS

BEANS: Brown, kidney, Mexican, pinto.

BOUQUETS: Aquavit, beer, brandy, lemon juice, sake, red vinegar, red wine, white vinegar, white wine, Worcestershire sauce.

CANDIES: Bitter chocolate, cocoa.

CONDIMENTS: Bitters, celery seed or salt, catsup, ground cumin, chili powder, chili sauce, cinnamon, curry powder, garlic juice, garlic powder, hickory smoke flavoring, horseradish (dry), pickling spices, salt, sugar (white and brown), Tabasco sauce, turmeric.

FATS: Bacon drippings, beef suet, butter, chicken fat, goose grease, lard, margarine, olive oil, vegetable and peanut oils.

FISH: Scallops.

FRUIT: Currant jelly, green olives, raisins, ripe olives.

GRAINS: Barley, rice.

HERBS: Basil, bay leaf, cloves, marjoram, oregano, sage, thyme.

MEATS: Bacon, beef, beef heart, chicken, corned beef, ham, lamb, mutton, pork, veal.

NUTS: Almonds, water chestnuts.

PASTA: Macaroni, spaghetti.

PEPPERS: Black pepper, cayenne, chili pods, jalapeño, melrose, Mexican, paprika, peppercorn, white pepper.

POWDERED MIXES: Baking soda, chili seasoning.

SAUCES AND BASES: Bean liquid, beef bouillon, beef stock, chicken gumbo soup, chicken stock, chili beef soup, onion soup.

THICKENINGS: Bread, cornmeal, cornstarch, flour, harina masa.

TOMATOES: Canned, garden, paste, juice, sauce, soup.

VEGETABLES: Carrots, celery, garlic, green onions, green peppers, mushrooms, parsley, pea pods, potatoes, purple onions, red peppers, Spanish onions, white onions.

A word about chili peppers:

The pungency of the burning capsicum is never lost, but the flavor can deteriorate as it loses color. So when shopping, try to get the reddest you can find.

Four pepper pods per pound of meat will provide a "very hot" Chili Con Carne. For milder chilis reduce the number in the proportion that will please you most.

Chili powder is a good substitute, though some of the "sting" of the fresh pod will be lost. Usually, a heaping tablespoon of chili powder will equal one average-size chili pepper.

BASIC CHILIS

BASIC CHILIS

No lovers of chili the editors have ever known confine themselves to a single recipe. It simply is fun to experiment when there is an infinite variety to be enjoyed. It is possible, too, that a modification made at home could become the rage of the neighborhood.

The editors have tasted chilis from Minnesota to Texas and from New York to California, in South America, the Orient, in Europe and the Mideast, and they state categorically that there is no superior way to make it. The addition of raisins may curl some people's hair; others may delight in the experiment. Pork or bacon may fit this occasion, ruin that one. The magic a cook puts into a dish one night might turn into a curse the next. Chili Con Carne is a subtle thing that changes with the maker. Imagine eating only Texas style chili for a lifetime, and then, God save us, trying to deflect the universal scorn and ridicule by bragging about it!

But there are plenty of armchair generals around with their multitude of "do's" and "don'ts" who should be promptly and rightfully ignored. Cooking the beans in the same pot? Excellent chilis are prepared not only in Amarillo but by Chasen's in Hollywood and at a little restaurant-bar in Valencia, Spain, by doing just that. Don't fry the onions with the meat, others say. But in *The Chili Cookbook* many splendid recipes say you must. Beef suet formerly was a necessary ingredient, but when the cholesterol scare began it was thrown out, even by experts, without much fuss.

The "basics" are to chili-making what the scales are to music. Once known, the various culinary tunes that can be played are endless. And they are yours to play with. But cooks, follow the recipes until you have mastered them! The coolest heads learn the anatomy of the "pure" or basic chilis — and *then* they perform their works of art.

The recipes that follow are termed "basic" because of their straightforward drive to the essence of the chili "taste." No flourishes, please! No distractions such as raisins or almonds. All of them are American or Mexican, not too hot, and require only minimum preparation. Some have been made in batches up to fifteen gallons for Chili Parties, which are famous in the Southwest.

MASA MASA *(Serves 4 to 5)*

A word about chili powder and masa. One of the best chili powders is Gebhardts's, made in San Antonio; it makes a difference. So does the masa, a Mexican maize ground fine as flour and containing a great flavor of corn. It is obtainable in Mexican stores and in some supermarkets.

1 cup dried pinto beans
3 tablespoons olive oil
1 medium onion, chopped fine
2 pounds stewing beef, diced into ½-inch cubes
3 cups water
3 tablespoons harina masa

4 tablespoons chili powder
1 teaspoon salt
1 teaspoon ground cumin
1 teaspoon oregano
2 tablespoons paprika
3 cloves garlic, chopped fine

1 bay leaf

Soak beans overnight. Add a sprinkle of salt after simmering two hours or until tender. Heat olive oil in a heavy iron skillet and sauté onion until soft. Add meat and sauté until gray, not brown. Add the water, turn up heat until water boils, then lower heat to simmer for one hour.

Next put masa, chili powder, salt, cumin, oregano, paprika, and garlic in a mixing bowl and add enough water to make a thin paste. Add this to the meat, drop in a bay leaf and simmer for another hour. Remove bay leaf, add whatever proportion of beans you prefer, heat together another five minutes and serve.

(Serves 12) LADY BIRD JOHNSON'S PEDERNALES RIVER SPECIAL

4 pounds chopped chili meat (venison or beef)
1 large onion, chopped
2 cloves garlic, finely chopped
1 teaspoon oregano
1 teaspoon ground cumin
6 teaspoons chili powder (more if you like it hotter)
2 cans (12 oz.) tomatoes
salt to taste
2 cups hot water

Put meat, onion and garlic into a large skillet and sear until lightly browned. Add all other ingredients. Bring to boil. Lower heat, cover and simmer one hour. Skim off grease and serve hot.

Lyndon Johnson used to say that when he was in Washington his kitchen shelves were crowded with cans of Texas chili "so I can survive the chili drought until I get home." Chili Con Carne in the White House? That is not so bad. It was said of Disraeli when he occupied 10 Downing Street, that he liked nothing better than American peanut butter on firm dark toast. Lady Bird Johnson's recipe, by the way, when it was in the *Saturday Evening Post,* received more requests for copies than a pamphlet on the care and feeding of children.

PANCHO VILLA *(Serves 4)*

Sometimes called "Connoisseur's Chili" because of its brash use of various peppers, this one goes back to the days of Pancho Villa and the great fiesta days at the Ranchito Granada when it was prepared by the ranchito's colorful mamacitas.

¼ cup olive oil
1½ pounds coarse ground (lean) beef
1 cup hot water
1 bay leaf
4 dry chili pods
1 teaspoon salt
3 cloves garlic, finely chopped

½ teaspoon ground cumin
½ teaspoon oregano or marjoram
½ teaspoon black pepper
¼ teaspoon red pepper
1 teaspoon sugar
1½ tablespoons flour
3 tablespoons cornmeal

Heat oil in deep frying pan and add meat. Stir continually until meat is seared gray, not brown. Add hot water, cover and let simmer for half an hour.

Add all other ingredients except flour and cornmeal. Let simmer another half-hour. Skim off fat. Mix flour and cornmeal in a little cold water and add to meat mixture. Cook another five minutes. Stir to prevent sticking, adding more water if needed.

SWEET SUET

Fat is beautiful but it can be dangerous, too. So be careful with this one if you are on a fat-restricted diet. For others, it is one of the best beef suet Chili Con Carne recipes ever dreamed up.

¼ pound beef suet, ground separately
4 pounds coarse ground chuck beef (fat left on)
2 medium onions, chopped
1 tablespoon salt
4 tablespoons chili powder, heaping
1 tablespoon ground cumin
1 teaspoon red pepper, crushed
¼ teaspoon sugar
1 garlic clove, crushed, or ½ teaspoon garlic powder

In a large, heavy pot render and brown the suet. Remove suet and add ground meat and chopped onions into its drippings. Stir constantly over medium heat until the meat is separated, gray in color and the onions are clear.

To the meat add salt, sugar, chili powder, red pepper, cumin and garlic and mix well. Add enough water to cover one inch above the meat mixture. Cover with a tight lid and let simmer one-and-a-half-hours. If meat appears dry during this time add more water. Taste for desired salt flavor.

Serve with cooked kidney or pinto beans this way: Spoon out the beans (sans liquid) into individual serving bowls, and then add the chili over the beans.

IT'S THE DICKENS *(Serves 6 or 7)*

What the dickens is it? It's Chili Con Carne and you'll find it's the dickens to make, but will prove to be well worth the trouble.

¼ cup olive oil

3 pounds (lean) beef, diced

1 can (16 oz.) tomato sauce

1 can (16 oz.) tomatoes

1 pint water

1 tablespoon chili powder

3 teaspoons salt

1 teaspoon garlic powder, or 8 cloves garlic, choppe

1 teaspoon ground cumin

1 teaspoon sugar

1 tablespoon paprika

1 teaspoon red pepper

6 tablespoons cornmeal

3 cans (16 oz.) kidney beans, drained

Heat olive oil in a six-quart pot, add meat and sear over high heat, stirring constantly until meat is gray, not brown. Add tomato sauce, tomatoes and water. Cover pot and cook at a bubbling simmer two hours. Add all spices and simmer an additional thirty minutes.

Fat will rise to the top after spices have been added; skim off according to your taste. Blend cornmeal with water to a pouring consistency, add to pot and cook at least five minutes more, stirring constantly to prevent sticking and to determine whether more water is necessary to bring to the consistency of Cream of Wheat. Add kidney beans and let simmer until beans are warmed through. This is medium hot chili. Feel free to vary the amount of chili powder for hotter or milder Chili Con Carne.

(Serves 2 or 3) A BIT OF MEXICO

A San Antonio writer, Charles Ramsdell, declares that "if Chili had come from Mexico, it would still be found there." Excuse us, sir, here is a Mexican chili dish you must have missed.

1 pound dry kidney beans (soak overnight)
1 tablespoon salt
1 pound beef and ¼ pound pork, ground together
1 tablespoon chili powder
4 dry chili peppers, ground up
2 large Mexican peppers, ground up (save seeds)
Take small seeds of the large peppers and add them to:
1 teaspoon ground cumin
1 teaspoon oregano (Mexican sage)

Tie seeds of the pepper, cumin and the oregano together in a cheesecloth bag. Cook beans separately, adding the one tablespoon salt after one hour. Cook all other ingredients (including seasoning bag) in hot water for an hour. Combine both pots and cook one hour longer.

THICK AND SASSY *(Serves 6 or 7)*

If you like thick Chili Con Carne, as they generally do in South America, you will be pleased with this one, in spite of its being practically drowned in garlic.

3 pounds coarse ground (lean) beef
¼ cup olive oil
1 quart water
4 bay leaves
8 dry chili peppers
3 teaspoons salt
10 cloves garlic, finely chopped

1 teaspoon ground cumin
1 teaspoon oregano or marjoram
1 teaspoon red pepper
½ teaspoon black pepper
1 tablespoon sugar
6 tablespoons cornmeal
3 tablespoons flour

Heat olive oil in a six-quart pot (cast-iron preferably) until it begins to smoke. Then add meat and stir constantly over high heat until meat is gray, not brown, and the consistency of whole grain corn. Add water and cook covered at a low simmer for one-and-a-half hours.

Now add all the ingredients except cornmeal and flour and stir well. Simmer another 30 minutes. Skim off fat. Add cornmeal and flour previously well-mixed in cold water, and stir well. Cook, stirring occasionally for five minutes. Remove bay leaves after the first half-hour of cooking.

(Serves 4 or 5) JALAPEÑO AUTHENTICO

Another genuine Mexican Chili Con Carne dish, this one uses that rarest of Mexican pepper, the jalapeño, which is available in many supermarkets and all Mexican groceries. Don't be shy; it's quite an experience.

1 medium onion (purple variety), sliced
4 cloves garlic, crushed
3 melrose peppers, sliced and seeded
1 jalapeño pepper, sliced, including juice and seeds
2 tablespoons goose grease or oil
2 pounds ground beef

1 teaspoon salt
1 teaspoon ground cumin
3 tablespoons chili powder
1 tablespoon paprika
¼ teaspoon cayenne pepper
½ teaspoon black pepper
4 cups water

Sauté onion, garlic, melrose peppers and jalapeño pepper with juice and seeds in grease until just tender. Then add beef and cook ten minutes until discolored. Add salt and all spices with water and cook two hours — longer if you want it thicker. Serve with pinto beans.

STOMACH WARMER *(Serves 3 or 4)*

This one is so good it may make you abandon all further experimentation on the subject. Though you will be happy, you will have lost the game. Try it, but keep your head!

1 large onion, chopped fine
1 clove garlic, minced
3 tablespoons cooking oil
½ pound beef heart, cut into ¼ inch cubes
½ pound ground (lean) beef
1 green pepper, finely chopped
1 can (20 oz.) tomato juice
1/8 teaspoon celery seed

½ teaspoon ground red pepper
½ teaspoon ground cumin
1 bay leaf, crushed
1 tablespoon chili powder, heaping
½ teaspoon salt
pinch of basil
2 cans (20 oz.) kidney beans, draine

Cook onion and garlic slowly in oil until onions are golden. Add beef heart cubes and ground beef. Stir frequently with fork so ground beef is broken up. Continue cooking until both ground beef and beef heart have lost their color, but are not brown.

Add all other ingredients except beans and simmer at low heat for two hours. Then add the beans and simmer for half an hour.

(Serves 5 or 6) RAPIDO

Other duties are always clamoring for your time. If Chili Con Carne pangs come upon you and you simply do not have time, here is a thirty to thirty-five minute recipe that is delicious.

1½ pounds ground beef
1 pound ground pork
½ pound ham
3 tablespoons olive oil
1 large green pepper, chopped
1 large onion, chopped
2 cans (8 oz.) tomato sauce

2 cups water
3 cans (16 oz.) kidney beans, drained
1 large bay leaf
1 teaspoon ground cumin
½ teaspoon chili pepper
1 tablespoon salt

Mix together beef, pork and ham and set aside. Heat olive oil in a casserole dish and then brown green pepper and onion, adding tomato sauce, bay leaf, cumin, chili powder and salt to make a Creole sauce. Add meat to this mixture and cook for ten minutes. Next add water and keep on cooking for another ten to fifteen minutes.

Finally, wash canned kidney beans well to remove sweet taste, add to casserole, cover and let stand until the flavors blend.

HOT PANTS STYLE *(Serves 6)*

Not to be eaten by people with high blood pressure, by actors just before filming a love scene, or by businessmen on the point of closing a deal.

¼ cup oil
3 pounds ground beef
1½ quarts water
4½ tablespoons chili powder
2½ teaspoons salt
8 cloves garlic, chopped
1 teaspoon ground cumin

1 teaspoon oregano
1 teaspoon cayenne pepper
½ teaspoon black pepper
1 tablespoon sugar
6 tablespoons cornmeal
1 can (8 oz.) kidney beans, drained

Heat oil, add meat and sear over high flame, stirring constantly until meat is gray, not brown. Add water and cook in covered pot at a bubbling simmer for one and a half hours.

Add all other ingredients except cornmeal and beans and cook another thirty minutes. Skim off most of the fat from the meat before thickening. Add cornmeal mixed with a little cold water and cook five minutes, to determine whether more water is necessary. Finally, add kidney beans, warm through, then serve.

SHADES OF TEXAS

Very fundamental and very simple, this is the way the range cooks made it, not having much room on the back of the chuck wagon for more than a stove and a pot. You''ll see what we mean.

2 pounds ground beef
5¼ cups water
1 tablespoon ground cumin seed
¼ cup chili powder
1 tablespoon crushed red pepper

1 tablespoon salt
5 cloves garlic, chopped
¼ cup oil
2 tablespoons flour
1 can (8 oz.) pinto beans, drained

Combine all ingredients in large pot with five cups of water, bring to boil and cook thirty minutes. Combine two tablespoons of flour with one-fourth cup water to make a paste. Add to chili, boil two minutes longer, add can of drained pinto beans and serve hot.

THE BROWN DERBY *(Serves 2)*

Simmering is the secret of this Chili Con Carne creation from the famous Hollywood restaurant. And it can be served with kidney or pinto beans, enchiladas or tamales.

¼ pound chopped beef suet
1 pound (lean) beef, chopped or ground
2 cups water
1 small onion, finely chopped
3 tablespoons chili powder
1 can (8 oz.) solid pack tomatoes
½ tablespoon paprika
½ tablespoon salt

Cook beef suet until melted, then add meat and water and simmer for one hour. Add onion and simmer another half hour. Add chili powder and simmer 30 minutes more. Add tomatoes and simmer one hour. Season with paprika and salt and stir well, then serve.

(Serves 6) DEEP BREATHER

One of the benefits of well-cooked peppers is the way they open clogged sinuses. This recipe is guaranteed to open more sinus cavities than have ever been opened before.

¼ cup olive oil
3 pounds coarse ground (lean) beef
1 quart water
6 tablespoons chili powder
10 cloves garlic, chopped fine
1 teaspoon oregano
½ teaspoon black pepper

2 teaspoons salt
1 teaspoon red pepper
1 tablespoon sugar
1 can (15½ oz.) kidney beans, drained
1 teaspoon ground cumin
3 tablespoons flour
6 tablespoons cornmeal

Heat olive oil, add meat, sear over high heat until gray, not brown. Add one quart of water and simmer in a covered pot for one and a half to two hours. Add all other ingredients except flour and cornmeal and let simmer for 30 minutes. Mix flour and cornmeal with a little cold water and add to pot, cooking five more minutes and adding more water if desired.

KID'S DELIGHT *(Serves 10 — or freeze some)*

For that big, boisterous birthday party, or any time the children bring a bunch home with them from school, make up a batch of this easy chili and see them glow.

4 chili pepper pods
2 quarts water
5 pounds ground beef
1 pound beef suet
1 bay leaf
½ can (3 oz.) tomato paste

pinch salt
2 onions, finely ground
4 cloves garlic, finely ground
1 teaspoon ground cumin
½ cup chili powder

Boil pepper pods in one pint of the water, then grind them down. Put everything together into a pot with remaining water, bring to boil and simmer for at least one and a half hours.

DAD'S FAVORITE

The use of vinegar in Chili Con Carne is quite unusual. Here it works well with paprika and provides just the right amount of *sting*.

2 cloves garlic, minced
1 large onion, minced
2 tablespoons chili powder
1 tablespoon paprika
¼ cup cooking oil

3 pounds round steak, chopped
1 can (16 oz.) tomatoes
salt and pepper to taste
2 tablespoons white vinegar

Put garlic, onion, chili powder and paprika into small container and mash with small wooden spoon until well blended. To this, add cooking oil slowly and mix well. Pour into skillet or pot and heat over low flame about five minutes.

Flour beef lightly and brown in the hot oil. Then add tomatoes, salt and pepper and cook over low heat for about one hour, stirring constantly, adding water if necessary.

After chili is thoroughly cooked, remove from heat and add vinegar. Good with oyster crackers or macaroni. Canned pinto or kidney beans may be added if desired.

LET IT STAND *(Serves 5 or 6)*

This may come as no surprise to some, but there is a Chili Con Carne that gets better with age. Like three days. If you have room in the fridge and the patience, you must try it.

3 pounds round steak, ground
1 can (1½ oz.) chili powder
1 large onion, chopped
4 cloves garlic, chopped fine
1½ tablespoons salt

2 tablespoons crushed red peppers
2 cans (6 oz.) tomato paste
3 cups hot water
dry red kidney beans, optional

Brown meat in large pot, stirring well so meat separates. Add chili powder, chopped onion and garlic. Add salt, red peppers, tomato paste and water. Bring to a boil and let simmer for three hours. Then let mixture stand for three days in the refrigerator, finally heating again before serving.

If beans are desired, use dry red beans. Let them stand fully covered in water overnight. In the same water bring them to a boil, then simmer until tender but *not overcooked,* (about one hour). Heat and serve in the chili.

(Serves 6) BLANCO'S RIO GRANDE

Horseradish did you say? Yes, there is a place for almost everything in Chili Con Carne, providing you know how to use it. Here is how to use that pungent root *Armoracia rusticana*.

½ pound beef suet, cut into small pieces
2 pounds round steak, ground and made into little balls
1 tablespoon turmeric
3 tablespoons dried horseradish, ground up
1 tablespoon salt

1 teaspoon white pepper
1 can (6 oz.) tomato paste
1 cup water
1 medium Bermuda onion, cut fine
3 tablespoons chili powder

Fry out beef suet in Dutch oven and add meat which has previously been braised. To seasonings, add one cup of water and put with the meat and suet, cooking slowly in the Dutch oven for one hour.

Serve with ground or chopped Bermuda onion and a bit of coarsely ground chili pepper sprinkled on top.

If pinto beans are added, they must be cooked separately.

A BED OF BEANS *(Serves 4 or 5)*

Here is another one that gets better with age. Kept covered in the fridge for a few days, it really m-e-l-l-o-w-s!

pinto or brown beans, prepared separately
½ pound beef suet
2 pounds ground beef
4 cloves garlic, chopped
4 tablespoons chili powder
1 tablespoon ground cumin
½ teaspoon cayenne pepper

1 teaspoon oregano
1 teaspoon salt
1 teaspoon sugar
1 can (16 oz.) tomato sauce,
   with 1 quart water
1 tablespoon cornmeal
1 tablespoon flour

Render suet and discard left-over fat. Add ground beef to renderings and stir until beef has turned brown. Lower flame and add garlic, all spices and sugar. Then transfer mixture to larger pot and add tomato sauce with one quart of water, simmering one hour, and stirring often.

Finally, mix the cornmeal and flour in half a cup of water and add to the chili for thickening. Remove from fire, cool and put into the refrigerator.

When ready to serve, put pinto or brown beans, that were cooked separately, into individual serving dishes. Heat chili and pour over beans. Serve.

PINTO BEAN CHILIS

PINTO BEAN CHILIS

What is a bean? How long has man survived on its benevolence? Are beans in fact "hard on digestion, and make troublesum dreams," as William Turner wrote in his *Herball (1551)*? Did Jack climb up a lima bean or was it a broad bean stalk in Leicestershire to find his castle and a giant on top?

These questions have puzzled legumographers for centuries. More than ten thousand varieties of beans, and each with a Latin name! No wonder so little sense has been made out of them until now.

Luckily for Chili Con Carne eaters, only three of the beans are important to know about. These are the Mexican or red, the pinto and the kidney bean. And since red and kidney beans are so much alike, *The Chili Cookbook* will deal mainly with pinto and kidney beans.

The pinto bean is far and away the most popular for chili dishes. It also is the most important bean in the world. A brown and white mottled bean that resembles the kidney in shape and size, it is grown extensively on the western slopes of the Rocky Mountains, in Colorado and in other southwestern states as a field bean for food and stock feed. Its growth habit is as a climber, as opposed to an erect bush. It is, like most beans, frost-tender and heat-tender, and Brazil, the United States and China produce more than half the world's supply of almost seven billion pounds a year.

The bean comes to us with a Spanish name, "pinto," which means "painted," or piebald or mottled. In China it is a staple food second only to rice in importance. Whether it is a good substitute for meat is a continuing debate.

In the opinion of the editors it is not, for it contains only sixty percent of meat's protein and lacks many of the body-building blocks provided by the amino acids found in meat. For dieters, pinto beans are the thing! They contain not more than four percent of fat calories. They also contain a high content of phosphorus, an essential mineral along with calcium for bones and teeth.

Some cooking points to remember: when beans are soaked in water their vitamin and mineral content passes into the water (especially that important phosphorus). So they should be cooked in the water in which they were soaked. A slow fire is best to keep the protein from getting tough. Add salt only after beans have become tender; salt attracts water away from the bean rather than into it.

For newcomers to bean cookery, here is a typical serving for four people, as well as the best pinto bean recipe the editors know.

2 cloves garlic, minced   *1 pound dried pinto beans*
1 teaspoon ground cumin   *3 slices bacon or salt pork*
1½ teaspoon salt   *2 small onions, chopped*

Soak beans overnight. Cut bacon into small pieces and cook in kettle that will hold beans. When cooked, add onions and garlic, stirring until the onions are wilted.

Pour beans in their soaking water into kettle and cook until almost tender (30 minutes). Then add cumin and salt and more water to cover beans about one inch. Bring to simmer until thoroughly tender (20 minutes more), then serve.

ONIONS AND STUFF *(Serves 4 to 6)*

Always on the lookout for the unusual pinch of this 'n' that in Chili Con Carne, the editors here present a recipe that is truly a cook's delight.

3 tablespoons olive oil
2 cups onions, finely chopped
2 cloves garlic, chopped
1 green pepper, chopped
1 pound round steak, ground
½ pound pork, ground
3 tablespoons chili powder
1 can (16 oz.) tomatoes
1 cup beef stock or water

½ teaspoon celery salt or seed
1 teaspoon ground cumin
pinch of oregano
½ teaspoon cayenne pepper
1 small bay leaf
1/8 teaspoon basil
1½ teaspoons salt
1 teaspoon sugar
2 cans (8 oz.) beans, drained

Heat oil in large saucepan and cook onions, garlic and green pepper until wilted. Add meat and cook until meat has lost its red color. Combine chili powder with this mixture.

Add tomatoes and half of the beef stock, then all the remaining spices, sugar and salt. Cook one to two hours, stirring occasionally. If necessary, add remaining beef stock. Stir in beans and serve.

CHASEN'S FAMOUS CHILI

(Serves 6 or 7)

To this Beverly Hills restaurant the swinging stars go to eat and be seen. And from Chasen's, Elizabeth Taylor had frozen chili flown to her during the shooting of *Cleopatra* in Rome.

½ pound dried pinto beans
2 cans (16 oz.) tomatoes
1 pound green peppers, seeded and coarsely chopped
1½ pounds onions, coarsely chopped
1½ tablespoons salad oil
2 cloves garlic, crushed
½ cup parsley, finely chopped

½ cup butter
2½ pounds ground chuck beef
1 pound ground (lean) pork
1/3 cup chili powder (2 more tablespoons will make it hotter)
2 tablespoons salt
1½ teaspoons pepper
1½ teaspoons ground cumin

Wash beans, place in bowl and add water to two inches above beans. Soak overnight. Simmer, covered, in the same water until tender. Add tomatoes and simmer five minutes. Sauté green peppers slowly in salad oil for five minutes. Add onion and cook until tender, stirring frequently. Add garlic and parsley.

In large skillet melt butter and sauté beef and pork for about fifteen minutes. Add meat to onion mixture, stir in the chili powder and cook ten minutes. Add this mixture to beans and season with salt, pepper and cumin, then simmer, covered, for one hour. Remove cover and cook thirty minutes longer. Skim fat off the top. This chili freezes beautifully.

CANNONADEER *(Serves 4)*

Little fuss and a lot of fun to this one. It's almost as simple as combine, cook and serve. You'll see.

3 cloves garlic, crushed
1 cup onions, chopped fine
2 tablespoons shortening
1½ pounds ground beef
1 pound ground pork
1 can (13 oz.) tomato purée or tomatoes
2 teaspoons salt

2 teaspoons oregano
1 tablespoon sugar
½ teaspoon ground cumin
¼ teaspoon cayenne pepper
1 tablespoon paprika
½ cup chili powder
1 can (16 oz.) pinto beans, drained

Cook garlic and onions in the shortening. Add meat and brown well. Add all other ingredients and simmer slowly until meat is done. One can of pinto beans, drained and heated through, suffices.

OLD CARNEY

Here is a Midwest version of Chili Con Carne, which has served some families for over forty years.

1 pound dried pinto beans, soaked overnight
3 medium onions, chopped
1½ cups olive oil
2 pounds ground round steak
1 pound ground (lean) pork
2 quarts boiling water
2 cans (8 oz.) tomato sauce
chili powder, garlic and salt to taste

Cook beans in water to cover for one hour, or until tender. Drain and set aside. Simmer onions in olive oil for ten minutes. Add beef and pork and simmer another twenty minutes, stirring frequently. Combine two quarts of boiling water, tomato sauce and seasonings with meat and cook one hour. Add beans, heat through and serve.

If you are tempted, but do not wish to risk all, wrap one teaspoon each of oregano and cumin in a piece of cheesecloth and add to chili during last half hour of cooking. This will add quite a bit to the taste.

THE SLY ONE (Serves 4)

Here is a Chili Con Carne that sneaks up on you. Plain as a sugar cookie and economical. But are sugar cookies and saving a penny necessarily bad?

1 pound dried pinto beans, soaked overnight
1 pound ground stewing meat
1 teaspoon salt
1 onion, chopped
1 tablespoon chili powder
1 can (6 oz.) tomato paste
2 tomato paste cans water

Soak beans overnight, then cook in water to cover one hour, or until tender. Brown meat, add salt, onion and chili powder and cook ten minutes. Mix tomato paste with water and add to beans in their own juice. Simmer half an hour until flavors blend.

SLIGHTLY SMASHED

If you like onions and tomatoes dominating everything, you will be mad about this recipe.

1 pound dried pinto beans, soaked overnight
1 teaspoon salt
2 medium white onions, diced
1 ounce peanut oil
1½ pounds coarse ground stewing beef
2 ounces ground cumin
2 ounces chili powder
1 clove garlic, mashed
2 cans (16 oz.) tomatoes

Soak beans overnight, cover with water, bring to a boil and simmer one hour or until tender. Add one teaspoon salt.

Brown onions in peanut oil. Add meat, cumin, chili powder and garlic. Cook until meat turns brown. Add tomatoes, cover and simmer one hour.

EVEN STEPHEN *(Serves 6 or 8)*

Here is a versatile Chili Con Carne that you can cook in a skillet or pot, or even bake. Whichever way, it will be good all the same.

2½ cups dried pinto beans, soaked overnight
2 teaspoons salt
2 tablespoons olive oil
1 cup onions, chopped
1 red pepper, chopped

1 clove garlic, chopped
1 pound ground beef
2½ cups tomatoes
1 tablespoon chili powder
½ teaspoon black pepper

Soak beans overnight, then cook in water to cover one hour, or until tender. Add one teaspoon salt and set aside. Drain before adding to chili. In olive oil, over low heat, add onions, pepper and garlic and sauté gently about two minutes. Crumble meat, add it and continue cooking until meat is slightly browned. Add remaining ingredients (except beans), cover and simmer over low heat two hours, or place in a slow oven (300 degrees) and bake two hours. Add beans about fifteen minutes before serving.

(Serves 6) THREE-HOUR BEANS

Needless to say, not everybody has the foresight to think about tomorrow's meal in time to put on a pan of beans to soak overnight. Here is a Chili Con Carne that is designed to disguise that malfeasance on the part of the family cook.

3 cups dried pinto beans
1 onion, chopped
2 cloves garlic
1½ pounds coarse ground beef
1 teaspoon red pepper, crushed
1 teaspoon black pepper

1 tablespoon salt
3 tablespoons ground cumin
1 ounce chili powder
1 can (20 oz.) tomatoes
1 quart beef stock
1 tablespoon oregano

Wash beans, cover with water and put to boil, adding more water as needed. Cook about two-and-one-half to three hours.

Chop onion and garlic fine and sauté in frying pan. Add meat and cook until brown. Then add red pepper, black pepper, salt, cumin and chili powder. Over medium flame, stir and blend. Transfer into a large pot and add tomatoes and beef stock. Bring to a boil, then simmer for one and a half hours. Add oregano and beans and serve.

TOGETHERNESS *(Serves 10)*

This one makes the Texas chili consortium so mad they forget to tend to their oil wells, because the beans are cooked with the meat. However, out Montana way and in Idaho and Utah, it's raved about. Just goes to show that on Chili Con Carne, of all subjects, one should keep an open mind.

4 cups dried pinto beans
3 quarts water
4 teaspoons salt
1 large onion, peeled
1 large bay leaf
1 garlic clove, sliced

2 pounds ground (lean) beef
1 medium onion, chopped fine
3 tablespoons shortening
3 tablespoons chili powder
1½ teaspoons ground cumin
2 cans (6 oz.) tomato paste

Boil beans in three quarts of water for two minutes. Remove from heat, cover tightly and let stand for one hour. Then add salt, the whole onion, bay leaf and garlic. Bring back to boiling point rapidly, reduce to simmer, cover again and simmer for two hours. Remove whole onion and bay leaf (it may take some fishing!).

Brown meat and chopped onion quickly in shortening and then mix in beans. Make a paste of chili powder, cumin and tomato paste with some liquid from the beans. Blend into bean mixture. Bring to boiling point again, reduce heat, cover tightly and simmer one to one and a half hours.

58

VEGETARIAN DREAMBOAT

Everybody to his own tastes or principles. And lest our brethren who abhor meat shall likewise abhor Chili Con Carne, here is one for them.

4 cups dried pinto beans	½ cup onion, chopped
6 cups lukewarm water	½ cup green pepper, chopped
4 teaspoons salt	2 cups bean liquid
½ cup oil	1½ teaspoons chili powder
1 clove garlic, chopped	½ teaspoon black pepper

Wash beans, add to water, cover and cook slowly until tender (about two hours). Add salt half an hour before beans are done. Drain off two cups of bean liquid and one cup of beans to save for making sauce. Before serving, turn beans into a hot serving dish, over which pour the following sauce:

Heat oil in skillet, add garlic, onion and green pepper. Cook until soft. Add a portion of beans and mash thoroughly, then add one cup of the bean liquid. Repeat this until cup of beans is used up. Cook until mixture is of desired thickness, add seasonings, and pour over beans in serving dish.

TAPS *(Serves 6)*

As the final pinto bean chili, here is a chowder-type dish which has as its highest recommendation that it comes from non-pinto bean country. specifically Oregon. One can't help but wonder what Texans will think of it.

3 cups dried pinto beans, soaked overnight
2 quarts cold water
1 pound ground chuck beef
½ cup olive oil
2 cups onions, minced

1 garlic clove, minced
2 tablespoons salt
¼ teaspoon cayenne pepper
4 teaspoons chili powder
3 cans (8 oz.) tomatoes

Wash and soak beans overnight. Cover and bring to a boil in the same water. Reduce heat, simmer until beans are easily puréed with a fork (about thirty minutes). Add all other ingredients and continue cooking, covered, until beans are tender and chili is the consistency of chowder (about one and a half hours).

KIDNEY BEAN CHILIS

KIDNEY BEAN CHILIS

A quotation from the Chinese (by Lin Wan Po, from his book *Building the Great Wall*, London, 1929), goes like this:

"The bean. The lowly bean. What is it about beans? Oh, the bean lacks style; the rich rarely eat them, pretentious cooks keep them off the menu. But the poor manage very well with them, given a pinch of salt and pepper. Poor despised bean — a blessed thing!"

The second most important bean in the world is the kidney. Of Central and South American origin, it has been grown for food since prehistoric times. It is known as well as the French or haricot bean *(Phaseolus vulgaris)*, and is similar in composition but differs widely in eating quality from the pinto. Definitely kidney-shaped, its coloring is red, dark red and sometimes even white.

It is discouraging for Chili Con Carne eaters to note, however, that of all beans the kidney is by far the most apt to cause dyspepsia. So what is the kidney bean lover to do? The answer lies in the cloves of garlic called for in most Chili Con Carne recipes. This marvelous bulb has a definite anti-dyspeptic effect when added in only small amounts to food that causes flatulence. Apparently the volatile components evaporating from freshly cut garlic exert a considerable inhibiting effect on the bacterium that causes the flatulence.

The answer was found in *The Encyclopedia of Common Diseases* published by the Rodale Press of Emmaus, Pennsylvania. Noting the work of Dr. Frederic-Camrau and chemist Edgar Ferguson in explaining why garlic relieves distress brought on by accumulation of gas, it quotes from a 1949 paper published in the Review of Gastroenterology. The two men call garlic a carminative; that is, an "aromatic or pungent drug, used in flatulence and colic, to expel gas from stomach and intestine, and to diminish the gripping pains."

So, Chili Con Carne eaters, inbuilt in the dish with kidney beans is its own relief — providing you use garlic whether the recipe calls for it or not. In addition, garlic is so excellent a food in its own right, containing many valuable nutrients, that its use can beneficially affect other parts of the body.

That "second most important bean in the world" may easily become the first when you are finished with this chapter. Here are fifteen recipes that show how vastly different the kidney bean is from the pinto. And, best of all, unlike the pinto bean recipes, all of them use the canned product which is every bit as good as those you would attempt to make yourself. Enjoy them!

ACCENT ON PEPPERCORNS (Serves 4 to 6)

This one you can make when you get home from work, on a day when that "passionate craving" has seized you. The peppercorn touch will delight you.

1 tablespoon melted butter
1 pound ground beef
1 large onion, diced
4 tablespoons chili powder

6 peppercorns
3 cans (8 oz.) tomato sauce
1 can (20 oz.) tomatoes
1 can (16 oz.) red kidney beans, with liquid

In the melted butter fry the ground beef and onion until onion is tender. Add chili powder, peppercorns and simmer a few minutes. Add tomato sauce, tomatoes and beans (do not drain). Simmer half an hour.

(Serves 4) MIDWEST CAYENNE

In Frank X. Tolbert's book, *A Bowl of Red*, the author quotes a letter from a man in Battle Creek, Michigan, which says: "Chili here is not much more than a mildly peppery tomato soup, and I yearn for the real thing." Here, then, is a real Midwest chili the letter writer might try.

2 tablespoons shortening
1 pound ground beef
2 onions, minced
1 clove garlic, minced
½ green pepper, diced
1 can (20 oz.) tomatoes

1 can (20 oz.) kidney beans (save liquid)
1 tablespoon salt
dash cayenne pepper
1½ tablespoons chili powder
1 cup water

Melt shortening in a heavy kettle, add ground beef and sear until brown. Add onions, garlic and green pepper and brown lightly. Stir in tomatoes, kidney beans with liquid, salt, cayenne pepper and chili powder and add water. Cover and cook slowly for one-and-one-half hours.

MUSHROOM SNIFFLE *(Serves 4)*

Who says "if it's easy it can't be good?" Here is one that not only is easy *AND* good, but can be doubled or tripled to please a bigger crowd without any effort at all.

1 pound ground chuck
1 can (16 oz.) tomato sauce
1 tablespoon chili powder
1 teaspoon salt

1 can (4 oz.) mushrooms and juice
1 teaspoon onion powder
1 can (20 oz.) kidney beans and juice
2/3 cup water

Brown meat until gray, not brown. Add remaining ingredients and simmer for a few minutes. It's done!

TEAR-JERKER

The name of this one honors the cook, who must chop up two cups of dry onions. But kidney beans and onions together make a good marriage, so it's worth trying.

4 tablespoons oil or fat	2 cans (10 oz.) tomato soup
2 cups onions, chopped	2 cans water
1 green pepper, diced	2 teaspoons sugar
1 clove garlic, chopped fine	2 teaspoons salt
1 cup celery, chopped	2 tablespoons chili powder
2 pounds ground (lean) beef	2 tablespoons warm water
1 can (16 oz.) tomatoes	2 cans (20 oz.) kidney beans, drained

Heat fat, add onions, peppers, garlic, celery and sauté until golden brown, then stir in meat until it browns. Add this mixture to a pan holding tomatoes, soup and water, sugar, salt, chili powder diluted with the two tablespoons of warm water, and cover and bring to a boil. Simmer slowly for about one hour. Add kidney beans and simmer an additional ten to fifteen minutes, serving hot.

FOR MILLIONAIRES ONLY (Serves 5 to 6)

Here is "haute cuisine" with a vengeance. "Top of the round" for Chili Con Carne? It calls for just that. The result is out of this world — and so is the cost.

1½ pounds ground top of the round steak
4 tablespoons oil
1 teaspoon red pepper, crushed
1 medium Spanish onion, finely chopped
1 bay leaf

4 cups boiling water
1 tablespoon chili powder
1½ teaspoons salt
2 cans (20 oz.) kidney beans, drained
1 tablespoon each of butter and flour

Sear ground meat in oil, add red pepper, onion, bay leaf and water. Simmer gently for one hour. Add chili powder, salt, and kidney beans and cook twenty more minutes.

Cream butter and flour and add slowly to mixture, cooking ten minutes longer.

Cooks in Colorado add their bit to the many-faceted chili feast. Here is the way they do it.

1½ pounds ground beef
3 tablespoons butter or oil
1 teaspoon salt
¼ teaspoon pepper
3 or 4 tablespoons chili powder

1½ tablespoons ground cumin
¼ cup flour
2 medium onions
1 large clove garlic
1 green pepper
1 can (6 oz.) tomato sauce

2 cans (20 oz.) kidney beans, or 1 can (16 oz.) pork and beans, with liquid

Cook meat in pot with oil. Add salt, pepper, chili powder and cumin. Cook and stir until meat loses its pink color. Sprinkle enough flour over meat to absorb grease and stir in. Add onions, garlic and green pepper which have been ground together in meat grinder (this also may be done in blender) with their juices. Add beans with liquid, two cans of water (one and a half if you use pork and beans), and tomato sauce. Cook for one hour, and serve.

THE S.S. JOHNNIE (Serves 6 to 8)

Here is the favorite of the crew of one of our Coast Guard destroyers which used to battle through the Atlantic during World War II. The addition of catsup may seem blasphemous, but that is the way the men liked it.

6 tablespoons shortening
3 pounds ground beef
1 quart onions, chopped
8 stalks celery, chopped
2 green peppers, chopped
3 cans (20 oz.) tomatoes
2 cups catsup

1 quart beef stock
1 tablespoon salt
1 teaspoon pepper
dash of Tabasco sauce
1 cup chili sauce
6 tablespoons chili powder
3 cans (8 oz.) kidney beans, drained

Heat about six tablespoons of shortening in a skillet and add beef, stirring until crumbly and brown. Add onions, celery and green peppers and cook until limp. Transfer into a large pot and add remaining ingredients, except beans. Simmer one-and-one-half hours. Add beans drained, cook fifteen minutes more, and serve.

IT'S PICKLED

Here is a Chili Con Carne that combines touches from Europe and South America, and is delicious served with rye bread and beer.

3 pounds coarsely ground beef
1 medium onion, diced
2 cans (16 oz.) tomatoes
1 tablespoon salt
pinch of black pepper
1 tablespoon paprika

1 teaspoon chili powder
½ teaspoon ground cumin
3 tablespoons mixed pickling spices
3 dried red peppers
2 cups water
2 cans (16 oz.) kidney beans, drained

Brown beef in heavy Dutch oven, then add onion, cooking until the onion is transparent. Add tomatoes to this mixture, then salt, pepper, paprika, chili powder and cumin. Measure out pickling spices, add the red peppers and put into a tea ball or tie into a cloth bag, which is dropped into the pot. Cover and simmer three to four hours, stirring occasionally to prevent scorching. Add water as needed. Finally, add beans, well drained, and cook fifteen minutes more.

PORKY *(Serves 4)*

Every variety of Chili Con Carne has its pork adherents, and here is one for kidney bean chili lovers.

¾ pound ground beef
¼ pound ground pork
1 tablespoon oil
1 large onion, chopped
1 green pepper, chopped
salt and pepper to taste

2 tablespoons chili powder
1 can (6 oz.) tomato paste
3 tomato paste cans of water
pinch of baking soda
1 bay leaf
1 can (20 oz.) kidney beans, drained

Brown meat in oil in heavy pot, then add onion and green pepper. Add salt, pepper and chili powder and cook ten minutes. Add remaining ingredients except beans, cover and simmer thirty minutes. Then add beans and simmer ten minutes longer.

(Serves 4 or 5) ADVENTURING

Here is another recipe using vinegar, that condiment which was never important in old Rome except for food preservation and, mixed with water, as a drink Roman soldiers took along on their marches. We of a later age are more adventurous, no?

1 medium onion, chopped
2 cloves garlic, chopped fine
1½ pounds beef, ground coarsely
1 tablespoon oil
6 teaspoons chili powder
1 teaspoon oregano
½ teaspoon marjoram
½ teaspoon sage

pinch of mustard
1 teaspoon sugar
1 can (20 oz.) tomatoes
1 can (8 oz.) tomato soup
1 bottle (8 oz.) chili sauce
2 teaspoons vinegar
2 cups (or more) water
2 cans (20 oz.) kidney beans, drained

Cook onion, garlic and meat in shortening until meat is slightly brown. Add other ingredients except beans. Lower heat and simmer about half an hour. Then drain beans, add them to mixture and cook another five minutes.

GREEN PEPPER *(Serves 5 or 6)*

Not a pepper but a vegetable, this rather mild "spice" was named by the Spaniards, who called any spicy edible they found in the New World a pepper. Here is a recipe green pepper lovers will really appreciate.

1½ pounds ground beef
1 ounce water
1 onion, diced
3 small green peppers, cut up
1 can (20 oz.) kidney beans, with liquid

1 can (16 oz.) tomatoes,
*   cut up, save juice*
1 tablespoon vinegar
½ tablespoon chili powder
salt and pepper to taste

Break beef into small pieces in a large pot or deep frying pan. Add one ounce of water. Let simmer. Add onion and green peppers and let simmer until meat turns brown. Add the beans and tomatoes with their juices and cook for one hour. Finally, add the vinegar and chili powder, season with salt and pepper to taste, and serve.

WATERFRONT

In almost any harbor town in the world, the national version of the chili parlor will be found. Here is a recipe familiar to many dock workers and sailors in the U.S.A.

2 pounds ground beef
¼ cup bacon drippings
1 can (16 oz.) tomatoes
1 large onion, chopped
1 tablespoon salt
1 tablespoon flour

1 teaspoon ground cumin
4 cloves garlic, minced fine
½ cup chili powder
1 tablespoon oregano
3 bay leaves, crushed
1 can (8 oz.) kidney beans, drained

Cook meat until brown in bacon drippings, stirring constantly. Rub tomatoes through a sieve into a pot. Mix everything else except beans together, and simmer for two hours. Add beans, cook another five minutes, and serve.

COMMUNAL *(Serves 6)*

From the ranching country of the far West, where life is less complicated than in our busy cities, comes this plain and excellent recipe. And it doubles or triples easily with no loss in taste.

2 pounds ground beef
1 medium onion, chopped
1 tablespoon salt
3 tablespoons chili powder
1 can (6 oz.) tomato paste
3 cups water
1 clove garlic, chopped
1 can (16 oz.) kidney beans, drained

Sear beef and onion. Add salt, chili powder, tomato paste, water and garlic, cover and simmer for three hours. Add beans just before serving.

(Serves 4) MINNESOTA STYLE

For all of their shouting about chili, here you will notice a greater resemblance to the real Aztec and Mayan Chili Con Carne than you will ever find in Houston.

1 clove garlic
1 teaspoon salt
¾ cup onions, chopped
2 tablespoons bacon drippings
1 pound ground beef
1 tablespoon flour
1/8 teaspoon black pepper

2 tablespoons chili powder
1 teaspoon oregano
1 can (20 oz.) kidney beans, drained
1 can (6 oz.) tomato paste
1 can (8 oz.) tomato sauce
1 cup water

Mash garlic with salt. Sauté onion in bacon drippings for five minutes. Add garlic and meat and cook about ten minutes, stirring frequently. Add flour, pepper, chili powder and oregano. Mix in remaining ingredients. Cook slowly, stirring occasionally, for one hour.

BREATHE EASY (Serves 5 or 6)

Remember what we said about garlic's effect on kidney beans? Here is a recipe that seems to have stumbled on the knowledge long before science figured it out. It's from South Dakota.

5 tablespoons shortening
6 cloves garlic, chopped
1 large onion, chopped
1 medium green pepper, chopped
2 pounds ground beef
2 cans (16 oz.) kidney beans with liquid
2 kidney bean cans water

1 can (16 oz.) tomatoes
1 can (6 oz.) tomato paste
2 tablespoons salt
2 teaspoons black pepper
1 can (1½ oz.) chili powder
2 chili peppers, crushed

In skillet or Dutch oven put shortening, garlic, onion and green pepper, and simmer five minutes. Add ground beef and scramble it through this mixture. Cook with cover on pot for five more minutes. Add beans and liquid and mix well. Then add water, tomatoes, tomato paste, salt and black pepper. Let this simmer half an hour. Then add chili powder and crushed chili peppers. Cook another half hour, stirring occasionally, and serve.

HOT CHILIS

"Although the tree is talling proud/He gives us only barkling wood/While the borning lowly chili plant/He gets our bodlings feeling good."

That charming song is sung on feast days by the peculiarly red-skinned natives of Eastern Malaysia. Similar folk tributes to the pepper plant *Capsicum frutescens* can be found in many corners of the world. For the little red fruit of the plant that gives Chili Con Carne its name has traveled far from its Indonesian home and its migrations have influenced social and cultural history around the earth.

Unknown to the Occident until the voyages of Columbus, when he brought back to Spain "pepper more pungent than that from the Caucus," by 1600 the burning capsicum was being cultivated in warmer climates around the world. Indonesia then and still does raise the hottest, but few reach Europe or America. Varieties grown in Central America and the West Indies were the source for the rich trade in peppers carried on through the seventeenth century, and led — since history so often follows publicity — to the erroneous conclusion, shared even by the *Encyclopedia Britannica,* that "they were America's most important contribution to the spices."

Today, most Chili Con Carne in America is made with capsicum grown in Mexico, California, New Mexico and Texas. A Japanese strain also is used. Called "Jap peppers," these are neither as colorful nor as hot as those grown here. Elsewhere in the world, the Mideast grows its own, as does southern China. In India the bulb is fat and pale red, as opposed to the slender red or purplish variety we know. Chili peppers can be grown in northern climates if treated as a tender summer annual: that is, cultivated the same as their relative, the tomato, with seeds sown under glass and the plantlets set out when weather permits.

Chili peppers generally are considered a condiment or spice without particular benefit to health. However, like the large, sweet pimiento which is a horticultural variety of the same species (and unlike black pepper, *Piperaceae,* which is from another family altogether) they are a rich source of both vitamins A and C, especially eaten as Mexicans eat them, straight from the wild state and like peanuts. The A is always retained in the canned or dried state of the pepper, but to a lesser degree when powered. About two-thirds of the ascorbic acid remains in canned or frozen peppers, but is lost completely when the pepper is dried. An active principle obtained from capsicum is used as a counterirritant in medicine, and to add pungency to ginger ale.

High color and the strength of the pepper go hand in hand, and either fresh whole peppers or dried ones freshly ground are best for Chili Con Carne. Third best are frozen peppers, and, lastly, powdered, because of the loss of vitamin A.

Now we come to the heart of what Chili Con Carne is all about, the heat treatment from the "grains of paradise" that the true chili lover cannot do without.

An interesting explanation of the "genial" glow invariably experienced after eating a bowl of very hot Chili Con Carne is as follows:

Chili peppers, say organoanalysts (who are experts in the theory of taste), have no taste, they merely *burn*. In texture, they *tingle* or feel *warm*. In effect, they register warmth through the nerves of various parts of the body. This burning produces dilation of the superficial blood vessels, which causes perspiration and brings about cooling as a consequence of the perspiration dry-off. Finally, the internal glow and tingle which follow may, in part, be pain, accompanied by local irritation but noted only vaguely because of the scarcity of taste receptors in the affected area.

As for the complaint of many people that chili peppers injure the taste buds because they are so hot, that is not true. The virility of the taste buds is lifelong. Continued stimulation may drive them to a fatigue point, and for a time increased amounts of the same substance may fail to raise the intensity of the taste sensation. But the taste-sensitivity of the buds is continually regenerated so that after a rest period of some seconds — or even minutes, depending on the amount of fatigue — the same buds again will respond to stimulation.

So, some like their Chili Con Carne very hot and that is neither good nor bad. That is the way the editors prefer it — and the hotter the better! In this chapter there are no "false alarms," as Wick Fowler, secretary of the International Chili Appreciation Society of Dallas, rates Chili Con Carne dishes.

In fact, most of them are at least "three alarm" or more. Here you will find "Fire Call," "Scorcher" and even "Inferno" chilis. And there may be found a lesson for you cooks who have never dared to go all the way. Like the famous Ollie of Fort Atkinson, Wisconsin, who used to throw chili parties for teen-agers who loved his cafe, you might find that the hotter you make it, the more your family and guests will rave about it. Keep your fire extinguisher handy, and good luck!

FIRE CALL *(Serves 6)*

Never let it be said that you are being pushed into the jaws of hell. This recipe will introduce you gently to the delights of "hot" Chili Con Carne without scaring you away by its surprising effects.

4 large onions, chopped
2 large green peppers, chopped
2 tablespoons oil
3 pounds ground beef
3 cans (16 oz.) kidney beans, drained

1 box (7½ oz.) chili powder
2 cans (16 oz.) tomatoes
4 tomato size cans water
salt and pepper to taste
pinch of ground chili pepper

Brown onions and green peppers in a little oil, add meat and brown. Then add rest of ingredients and simmer for two hours.

(Serves 9 or 10) NO EXIT

Get several strong characters together and spring this on them. The pork and Parmesan cheese make a most unusual combination.

2 pounds pork sausage, ground
1½ tablespoons paprika
3 tablespoons chili powder
1½ tablespoons cayenne pepper
1½ teaspoons black pepper
2 tablespoons salt
1½ tablespoons red pepper
1½ tablespoons dry mustard

5 small chili peppers
2 cloves garlic, cut up
1 tablespoon suet or lard
½ pound Parmesan cheese
4 cans (6 oz.) tomato soup
2 to 4 cups water
3 cans (16 oz.) kidney beans, with liquid

Put meat, paprika, chili powder, cayenne pepper, black pepper, salt, red pepper and dry mustard into skillet and sear until meat is lightly browned. In another pan take chili peppers, garlic and with one tablespoon of suet or lard sauté until tender. To this add the Parmesan cheese and cook until cheese melts and is thoroughly mixed with the garlic and peppers. Add this to meat mixture and stir together.

Then add tomato soup and water, simmering for one hour. About ten minutes before removing from fire add kidney beans with juice, heat through and serve.

SCORCHER *(Serves 6 or 8)*

We reach back to the ranches of Mexico for this one, which is easy to prepare but still shows those little touches that prove cooking can be an art.

3 pounds lean beef, coarsely ground
½ cup olive oil
1 quart water
8 chili peppers
3 teaspoons salt
1 teaspoon ground cumin
1 teaspoon oregano

1 teaspoon red pepper
10 cloves garlic, minced
1 tablespoon sugar
2 bay leaves
3 tablespoons flour
6 tablespoons cornmeal

In a large kettle fry meat in oil until dark brown. Then add one quart of water, cover and simmer for two hours.

Add remaining ingredients except flour and cornmeal and cook at a gentle simmer for thirty minutes, removing bay leaves after fifteen minutes. Make a paste of flour, cornmeal and water and stir into mixture, cooking another five minutes at a simmer while stirring often.

VOLCANO

This one is a favorite of the hill people who live in the Appalachian region of the United States, who always seem to have a pot of it bubbling on Saturday nights after dances in town.

1 large onion, chopped
1 clove garlic, minced
2 tablespoons oil
3 pounds ground beef
1 pound ground pork
2 teaspoons salt

1 teaspoon black pepper
1 can (1½ oz.) chili powder
2 tablespoons ground cumin
1 can (6 oz.) tomato paste
2 cups water
3 cans (16 oz.) kidney beans, drained

Fry onion and garlic in oil, then add meat, salt and pepper and sauté over a low heat. Add chili powder, cumin and tomato paste and water and cook slowly for one hour. Add kidney beans and cook one hour.

HOT PORKER *(Serves 4 or 6)*

The co-editors have had an argument over this one. Obviously, it is not the "hottest" chili in the world. Yet there are not many Chili Con Carne recipes that use bacon. In Iceland where it comes from, it is considered a rather daring dish. Maybe you can help us decide where it belongs.

½ *pound bacon*	*1 teaspoon salt*
1 green pepper, cut up	*1 teaspoon cayenne pepper*
1 large onion, diced	*1 can (20 oz.) tomato juice*
1 clove garlic, crushed	*1 can (6 oz.) tomato paste*
1 pound ground beef	*1 cup hot water*
1 tablespoon chili powder	*1 can (16 oz.) kidney beans, drained*

Cut bacon into small pieces and fry until slightly brown. Add green pepper, onion and garlic and cook slowly, stirring occasionally, until onion is seared. Add meat and stir until it is separated and slightly browned. Add seasonings and stir. Then add tomato juice and tomato paste and water, and simmer for thirty minutes. Finally, add beans and cook ten minutes longer.

(Serves 6) # HELL'S FIRE

Your blender gets a workout with this one. And "blending" is this recipes' secret. The way it folds in the flavor of the tomatoes and the chili peppers makes all the difference.

1 pound dried pinto beans
1 clove garlic, whole
1 teaspoon salt
2 pounds ground beef
1 tablespoon butter
1 can (20 oz.) tomatoes, whole
4 chili peppers

Soak pinto beans overnight. Then simmer in enough water to cover, add garlic and salt and cook until tender.

Brown beef in butter. Put tomatoes into blender. Remove veins and seeds from pepper and toast peppers in a frying pan, turning often. Add peppers to tomatoes and blend until liquified. Add to beef and simmer ten minutes. Remove garlic from beans, then add beans and some of the bean liquid until chili is the desired thickness. Heat through and serve.

NO RETREAT *(Serves 6 or 7)*

Lots of onions, lots of garlic and lots of peppers. This one is not for children nor is it for the chicken-hearted.

1½ pounds beef suet
3 pounds ground beef
6 onions, chopped fine
4 cloves garlic, chopped fine
½ dozen chili peppers, cut up
1 can (1½ oz.) chili powder
2 tablespoons ground cumin
4 cans (8 oz.) kidney beans, drained

Render suet and add meat, onions and garlic, and brown. Add enough water to cover meat and simmer for one hour. Add peppers which have been soaked in hot water, and use pepper water, too. Add spices and cook slowly until the mixture thickens. Add beans and heat through.

(Serves 4 or 6) WHEN AUTUMN COMES

On that Saturday or Sunday afternoon when "Dad and Son" come home from a football game, why not have this little "fireplace" going for them?

4 red onions, chopped
2 cloves garlic, chopped
½ cup oil
2 pounds round steak, coarsely ground
3½ teaspoons chili powder
4 tablespoons ground cumin
2 chili peppers
1 can (16 oz.) kidney beans, drained
4 cups water

Sauté chopped onions and garlic in one-half cup of oil. Add meat and cook until brown. Add chili powder, cumin and chili peppers. Add beans and four cups of water, and simmer an additional thirty minutes before serving.

INFERNO *(Serves 9 to 10)*

Here is one of the best "Chili Mac" recipes we know, and it was found not in Texas but in a little restaurant on lower Third Avenue in New York City.

2 cups dried kidney beans
3 pounds ground beef
2 cups water
2 cans (20 oz.) tomatoes
3 cups onions, chopped
4 cloves garlic, minced
4 teaspoons salt

5 tablespoons chili powder
2 tablespoons paprika
4 chili peppers
1 teaspoon thyme
2 teaspoons sage
2 tablespoons cider vinegar
2 boxes elbow macaroni

Soak beans overnight and drain. Brown meat in skillet, add beans, water, tomatoes, onions, garlic and seasonings. Cover and cook slowly for about five hours. The last half hour add vinegar. Cook macaroni separately, add and serve.

CHUNKY CHILIS

That there is a difference between Chili Con Carne made with ground beef and that made with cubes, hunks, or shreds of beef has an ancient tradition to back it up.

One of the Eight Immortal Dining Pleasures of the early Kamakura period (1185-1333) of Japan was "body" as applied to food, by which was meant those morsels of food that required biting-into, preliminary to chewing.

The sage Eisai (1141-1215) recorded in one of the early Zen works he and other Japanese monks brought back from China (Zen in Chinese is Ch'an) that the act of slicing through a piece of food with the front, or incisor, teeth, gave pleasure roughly equal to the flavor of the food itself, and a good measure of the expertise of the cook was how many of these *bitable* substances were contained in a meal. Hence the crispness of so many Japanese and Chinese cooked vegetables. Chewing, Eisai maintained — the act of crunching, tearing, masticating and preparing food for passage to the stomach — was merely accessory machine work and tiring, dull and vulgar.

According to organoanalysts, "bite," or the texture of food, definitely affects flavor. Their explanation for this is that a texture that is unusual inhibits the normal senses of taste and smell and becomes dominant as an element of the taste. Lin Yutang wrote that the Chinese "eat food for its *texture*, for the elastic or crisp effect it has on the teeth, as well as for fragrance, flavor and color."

And likewise with Chili Con Carne lovers who make chunky chilis a way of life. Ground meat is just not used, they say. It is like cooking with sawdust! Any meat — beef, venison, pork or even lamb — will do, but it must be shredded or cubed, never ground, to get that special thing called "bite."

Putting it tersely, the authors herewith present a proposition concerning the act of eating.

Food:
Dumb dogs gulp,
Smart cats bite.
You might
Take a cue:
Bite too.

Enough said?

SIRLOIN AND RICE *(Serves 6)*

Here is another expensive one. But if you want steak to "bite" on, it might as well be top grade, right?

2 pounds sirloin steak
2 cups diced onion
1 cup green pepper, diced
2 cloves garlic, crushed
2 tablespoons vegetable oil
1 chili pepper
1 tablespoon salt

1 tablespoon paprika
4 tablespoons chili powder
Tabasco sauce to taste
2 cans (20 oz.) tomatoes with juice
2 cans (8 oz.) mushrooms, drained
1 can (4 oz.) black olives, drained and sliced
2 cans (16 oz.) kidney beans, drained

Broil steak to medium rare, season and set aside.
Sauté onions, green pepper and garlic in vegetable oil until golden brown, then add all other ingredients .
Cut steak into two-inch strips and add to chili. Bring to a boil, then simmer for at least one and a half hours, skimming off excess fat and stirring occasionally. Then serve in bowls with a side dish of rice, garlic bread and green salad.

(Serves 6) ALLEGHENY HIGHWAY

We found this one in a roadside restaurant just outside of Charleston, West Virginia. The owner-cook, a raw-boned and handsome woman, remarked after we had each eaten two bowls that she was surprised damn Yankees would know a good chili when they found one.

2 pounds beef
2 tablespoons chili powder
2 cloves garlic, minced
3 tablespoons flour
¼ cup fat

2 tablespoons chopped suet
1 large onion, minced
2 teaspoons salt
1½ quarts hot water
1 can (20 oz.) kidney beans, drained

Cut up beef in chunks and toss it with chili powder, garlic and flour. Melt fat and suet together in a Dutch oven, then fry onion in the Dutch oven until tender. Add meat mixture. Cook for fifteen minutes. Add salt, pour on hot water slowly and simmer for forty-five minutes. Add beans, heat thoroughly and serve.

NO TOMATOES, PLEASE! *(Serves 8 to 10)*

Getting back to Texas and their abhorrence of tomatoes in Chili Con Carne, here is another version of the so-called "original Texas-style chili."

3 pounds lean beef
1 onion, chopped fine
2 tablespoons shortening
2 cloves garlic, minced fine
¾ teaspoon chili pepper
3 tablespoons chili powder

1 tablespoon ground cumin
¾ teaspoon paprika
2 teaspoons salt
dash of oregano
2 cups water

Cut beef into uneven little chunks. Sauté onion in shortening, then add meat, garlic, chili powder and ground cumin. Cook until meat is no longer pink. Add all remaining ingredients and simmer for two hours over low heat.

(Serves 3 or 4) CINNAMON FLAVORED

From El Paso and the children of the poor comes this hearty dish of Chili Con Carne, filled with vitamins.

3 cups dried pinto beans
1 onion, chopped fine
¼ pound salt pork
2 tablespoons chili sauce
¼ clove garlic, put through press
1 teaspoon smoke flavoring
¾ teaspoon cinnamon
salt and pepper to taste

Wash beans and simmer slowly with all other ingredients for five hours (cover beans with water to start and add water during cooking when necessary).

BOUILLON AND MUSHROOMS (Serves to 6)

Are you wondering "What will I do with my steak tonight?" Here is an answer discovered in Columbus, Ohio, that is sure to please the family.

2 onions, minced
1 green pepper, minced
4 tablespoons butter
1 pound round steak,
trimmed and cubed
4 celery stalks, minced
1 teaspoon chili powder

1 bottle (8 oz.) chili sauce
3 tablespoons catsup
1 tablespoon Worcestershire sauce
3 beef bouillon cubes
1 can (16 oz.) kidney beans, drained
1 can (4 oz.) button mushrooms, drained

Fry onions and pepper in butter, add meat and brown. Add remaining ingredients except beans and mushrooms. Simmer about one to one-and-a-half hours or until meat is done. When meat is done add beans and mushrooms (and some water if it has boiled down). Heat beans and mushrooms through and serve.

(Serves 6) OFF THE FARM

The wife of a poet friend served this Chili Con Carne one October day when we visited them on their farm in Wisconsin. Her use of pork shoulder with the beef was a very nice "bite" surprise.

2 tablespoons bacon drippings
1 large onion, minced fine
8 cloves garlic, minced fine
2 pounds beef, cut in cubes
1 pound pork shoulder, cubed
1 can (20 oz.) tomatoes, sieved
1 tablespoon salt

1 tablespoon oregano
3 small bay leaves
6 tablespoons chili powder
1 tablespoon flour
1 cup ripe olives, minced
½ cup water
2 cans (16 oz.) kidney beans, drained

Melt bacon drippings in a heavy skillet and add onion, garlic, beef and pork. Brown meat on all sides, cover and allow to steam about twenty minutes. Then add tomatoes, salt, oregano, bay leaves and chili powder mixed in a bit of water with flour. Simmer for one and one half hours. Then add olives, water, kidney beans, and simmer thirty minutes longer, adding more water if necessary.

ON THE PATIO *(Serves 5 or 6)*

Ripe olives have the effect of bringing chili down a bit from its sharp tang.
Here is another recipe that uses them generously.

2 pounds chuck or round steak
1 large onion, chopped
½ cup bacon drippings
1 can (28 oz.) tomatoes
1 pint ripe olives, cut up
1 can (20 oz.) kidney beans, drained
4 cloves garlic, minced fine

1 tablespoon salt
1 tablespoon flour
1 teaspoon ground cumin
¼ cup chili powder
1 tablespoon oregano
2 bay leaves, crushed

Cut meat into one-inch cubes. Sauté meat and onion five minutes in bacon drippings. Rub tomatoes through a sieve and add with all other ingredients except olives and beans to the meat mixture. Simmer for two hours. Add olives, then beans, heat through and serve.

(Serves 6) COCOA FLAVORED

Here is an unusual Chili Con Carne that has just about everything — wheat flour, sugar, cocoa — and red wine! It was found, of all places, in the Midwest.

3 cups pinto beans, soaked overnight
1 teaspoon salt
2 pounds beef, cut up
½ cup wheat flour
1 large onion, chopped
1 green pepper, chopped
salt to taste

4 large fresh tomatoes, peeled
1 teaspoon sugar
1 teaspoon ground cumin
2 tablespoons chili powder
1½ teaspoons cocoa
1 cup red wine
2 cups water

Cook beans in water to cover 1 hour, or until tender. Add 1 teaspoon salt and set aside. Drain before combining with chili.

Knead flour into beef. Brown in heavy skillet. Add onion, pepper and salt and cook about fifteen minutes.

Sprinkle tomatoes with sugar, and add to mixture. Then add all the remaining ingredients except beans and cover and simmer for two hours. Add beans and heat through. Serve hot.

AZTECA *(Serves 8)*

Observe in this ancient recipe made with tasty pinto beans when the salt goes in. It is an old Aztec trick known long before modern science proved it, that since salt tends to harden beans, *it must go into bean cookery last.*

1 pound dry pinto beans
2 pounds (lean) stew beef, cut into ¾ inch cubes
2 bay leaves
2 large onions, sliced
1 clove garlic, minced
2 tablespoons bacon fat
5 tomatoes

2 teaspoons salt
1 tablespoon cornstarch or 2 tablespoons cornmeal
¼ teaspoon dried oregano
¼ teaspoon sage
¼ teaspoon ground cumin
1 tablespoon chili powder (or more to taste)
1½ teaspoons black pepper

Soak beans overnight. Then put beans and meat on to cook together and when they are boiling vigorously add bay leaves, onions and garlic. The beans should be tender in one hour. At that time, heat up a skillet and add bacon fat, tomatoes, salt and cornmeal or cornstarch and rest of seasonings. Mix thoroughly and cook for five minutes, then add to beans and simmer another hour.

TRUCK STOP

This one you will find almost anywhere that hungry truck drivers stop to eat along Route #1. Plain, tasty and filling, for all we know it may be the Universal Truck Stop Chili.

1 pound pinto beans
3 tablespoons vegetable oil
4½ pounds chuck, cut in cubes
1 large onion, coarsely ground
4 cloves garlic, finely chopped
1/3 cup flour

5 tablespoons chili powder
2 teaspoons oregano
2 teaspoons ground cumin
3½ cups beef broth
salt to taste
fresh ground black pepper to taste

Soak beans overnight and then cook them until tender, about one hour. Slowly heat oil in a large saucepan, add beef and toss around in oil until it is gray. Add onion and garlic and toss around until onion is transparent. Mix together flour, chili powder, oregano and cumin, and sprinkle over meat cubes while stirring. Stir in beef broth, add salt and pepper and simmer slowly for about three hours until meat is fork tender. Add beans separately to each serving.

WHEELER-DEALER *(Serves 8 to 10)*

There is a restaurant in Springfield, Illinois, the state capital, where this recipe is made fresh every day the legislature is in session. And in the "genial glow" it produces, what big "deals" are made!

1½ to 2 cups pinto beans
¼ cup olive oil
2½ to 3 pounds lean beef, cut up
7 cups water
6 to 12 cloves garlic, diced
1 tablespoon sugar

1 teaspoon ground cumin
1 teaspoon marjoram
¼ cup paprika
3 tablespoons chili powder
4 teaspoons salt
¼ cup cornstarch

In a separate pan put beans and plenty of water. Cover and simmer until tender, about one hour. Rinse several times.

Heat oil in a large Dutch oven. Put beef into the smoking pot and sear, stirring until browned. Add 6 of the 7 cups of water and bring to a simmer. Add garlic, cover and simmer for one-and-one-half to two hours.

Add rest of seasonings to beef mixture and simmer, uncovered for forty-five minutes. Then add cooked beans and bring back to a simmer. Mix cornstarch into remaining cup of water and stir it slowly into chili until it thickens, then serve.

Here is a variation from west of the Mississippi — Grinnell, Iowa, in fact — that is so good it could conceivably interest even a Texan.

2 cups pinto beans
¼ cup vegetable oil
1 teaspoon garlic, finely chopped
1½ pounds chuck, chopped
2 teaspoons salt

¼ teaspoon white pepper
1½ tablespoons ground cumin
3 tablespoons chili powder
2 cups tomato soup
2 dashes Tabasco sauce

Soak beans overnight and cook separately until tender, about one hour. Heat oil, add garlic and meat, cooking slowly until meat is well done. Add salt, pepper, cumin and chili powder and cook for twelve minutes. Then add tomato soup, beans, hot sauce and enough water to make chili the consistency you prefer and simmer about thirty minutes.

A LA SPAGHETTI *(Serves 6 to 8)*

If there is a taste for "Chili Mac," there is bound to be one for "Chili Spag," and here is the only recipe for it we have ever seen.

½ cup olive oil
2½ pounds top round steak, cut in cubes
½ pound beef suet
1 cup onions, minced
2 medium cloves garlic, chopped
2 tablespoons chili powder
1 tablespoon paprika

1 tablespoon oregano
1 tablespoon ground cumin
1 teaspoon salt
½ teaspoon black pepper
1 to 2 cups water
1 can (12 oz.) kidney beans, drained
2 ounces cooked spaghetti

Heat olive oil. Add meat and suet and cook until meat is brown. Add onions and garlic and cook ten minutes over a low flame, stirring constantly. Stir in chili powder, paprika, oregano, cumin, salt and pepper. Add water and simmer until meat is tender. Add kidney beans and spaghetti, simmer until spaghett is tender, and serve.

BY ANY OTHER NAME

This recipe is as old as Mexico City itself, where it is translated as "Mexican Stew." Again, the word "chili" is a Texas invention and the dish is not known as that south of the border.

2½ pounds round or sirloin steak, diced
½ pound stew meat, diced
½ pound ground beef
salt and pepper to taste
1 tablespoon paprika

pinch dried marjoram
1 cup onions, chopped
2 cloves garlic, finely minced
1 tablespoon chili powder, or more
1 can (16 oz.) kidney beans and liquid

Season meat with salt and pepper and cook in a skillet until well browned. Add seasonings and liquid from beans. Cover and simmer gently until the meat is tender. Add kidney beans and more water if necessary and cook until the beans are heated through.

DASH OF CURRY *(Serves 6)*

No collection of Chili Con Carne recipes would be complete without one that uses this famous East Indian spice. Together with the garlic, what odors waft through the house!

2 onions, chopped
1 clove garlic, chopped
1 tablespoon butter
2 pounds beef, chopped
1 can (20 oz.) tomatoes
2 large chili peppers, chopped
1 large red pepper, chopped

1 tablespoon curry powder
1 tablespoon celery seed,
or one cup chopped celery
1 tablespoon salt
1 teaspoon cayenne pepper
1 can (16 oz.) kidney beans, drained

Fry onions and garlic in butter until tender. Remove and set aside. Fry meat in a kettle until brown, then add onions, garlic, tomatoes, peppers, curry powder and celery seed or celery, salt and cayenne pepper. Cook at a simmer for forty-five minutes. Then add drained beans and heat beans through.

CONVENIENCE CHILIS

CONVENIENCE CHILIS

Among the many myths that surround the American kitchen is that old saw of protogourmets that shortcuts in cooking are ill-advised.

On the contrary, shortcuts utilizing ready-made products such as canned or pre-mix foods may be just what your doctor ordered. Precisely because, through improvements in techniques, today's canned goods retain more vitamins than the ordinary cook can retain in the kitchen.

For example, canning techniques have little effect on protein, carbohydrates and fats. In general, vitamin A and pro-vitamin A (carotene) are not affected by the heat treatment given canned foods, whereas overcooking in many home kitchens destroys them. Vitamin D and riboflavin likewise remain intact. And vitamin C, that most evanescent of all vitamins, which is swiftly destroyed by atmospheric oxygen, is protected in the vacuum sealing of a can and is therefore retained.

So, harried contemporaries, the "convenience chilis" section is included in *The Chili Cookbook* for those who get that "passionate yearning" for chili when time is short but they still wish to prepare their own. The editors have tried them all and pronounce them better than passable, some unique, in fact.

In the following pages you will find fourteen of the easiest ways to prepare Chili Con Carne. Some take as little as five minutes to cook; few take longer than one hour. And all are good for the kids' lunch or their gang after school, good to prepare quickly at the Tupperware or Avon party in your house, or good for dinner when you come home late from work.

(Serves 2 or 3)

This is not the easiest in the book — that one will be found among the Odd Fellows — but it certainly comes close.

½ pound ground beef
¼ onion, minced
½ teaspoon salt
2 cans (8 oz.) chili beef soup
5 ounces water
chili powder to taste

Brown beef and onion in skillet with salt on the bottom, rather than oil. Pour off unwanted fat from meat, add the chili beef soup and water and stir until smooth. Add chili powder and simmer three or four minutes. A green salad and oyster crackers go good with this one!

EASY DOES IT *(Serves 6)*

The beans in this recipe make it a bit of a bother. Otherwise, the grocer practically makes it for you.

1 pound kidney or pinto beans
bacon fat or ham chunks
1 large onion, chopped
1½ pounds ground fatty chuck
1 can (20 oz.) tomatoes
1 can (16 oz.) tomato sauce,
or 2 cans (6 oz.) tomato paste

1 package chili seasoning
½ teaspoon oregano
½ tablespoon ground cumin
½ teaspoon sugar
salt and pepper to taste
water as necessary

Soak beans overnight. Cook in enough water to cover, adding bacon fat or ham chunks, if desired, until tender.

Fry onion in bacon fat, add meat and brown. Add remaining ingredients and simmer thirty minutes. Serve with beans.

SPONTANEOUS

Save the tops of green onions to use in this recipe. They are loaded with vitamins and the fragrance they impart to the brew is out of this world!

2 pounds ground beef
3 cloves garlic, mashed
1 cup green onions, chopped with tops
2 tablespoons butter
2 cans (16 oz.) kidney beans, drained
1½ tablespoons paprika

3 tablespoons chili powder
1 teaspoon salt
1 teaspoon white pepper
1 can (8 oz.) condensed onion soup
1 can (8 oz.) beef bouillon
1 soup can water

Place ground beef, garlic and onions in skillet with two tablespoons of butter. Sear until meat is light brown. Add other ingredients and bring to a boil. Lower heat, cover and simmer for twenty minutes.

(Serves 4)

This one is a little on the mild side. If you are one of those who prefer your Chili Con Carne that way, it is made to order for you.

1 pound ground beef
1 onion, chopped
1 tablespoon fat
1 can (16 oz.) kidney beans, drained
1 can (8 oz.) tomato juice
1 teaspoon salt
1/8 teaspoon black pepper
dash of cayenne pepper
½ tablespoon chili powder

Cook meat and onions in the fat until the meat is lightly browned. Add remaining ingredients and simmer gently for fifteen to twenty minutes.

(Serves 6 to 8)

The cut up bacon bits in this one is a quaint touch you might like to adapt now and then to other recipes in this book.

6 slices bacon, cut up fine
1 pound veal and 1 pound
   pork, ground together
1 can (20 oz.) tomatoes
2 green peppers, diced
2 large onions, diced

1 can (16 oz.) kidney beans, drained
1 teaspoon salt
½ teaspoon chili pepper, ground
½ teaspoon chili powder
tomato juice (if desired) for thinning

Fry bacon bits until light brown, add veal and pork and simmer fifteen minutes. Add tomatoes and simmer fifteen more minutes. Add green peppers, onions and beans and simmer another fifteen minutes. Add salt, chili pepper and chili powder, simmer ten minutes, and serve.

RING-AROUND (Serves 4)

Here is a different way to serve Chili Con Carne — in a ring of spaghetti. But how do you make a spaghetti ring? It will be explained below.

1 medium onion, chopped
1 small clove garlic, minced
1 tablespoon margarine or bacon drippings
1 pound ground beef
2 cans (16 oz.) kidney beans, drained

1 can (8 oz.) tomato soup
1 soup can water
1 teaspoon salt
1 tablespoon chili powder
chili peppers to taste

Sauté onion and garlic in margarine or bacon drippings until light yellow in color. Add meat and cook until lightly browned, stirring constantly. Add kidney beans, soup, water, salt, chili powder and peppers and simmer thirty minutes.

To make spaghetti ring, boil desired amount of spaghetti until tender. Pack firmly into greased round mold and unmold at once on platter to keep hot for serving.

(Serves 4 to 5) DEXTEROUS

This one turns out to be great if you carry your lunch to work and have a thermos. With seashell macaroni added, it's a fine noonday meal.

2 pounds ground beef
1 large onion, chopped
2 cloves garlic, chopped
2 cans (16 oz.) kidney beans, drained
1 can (8 oz.) tomato soup (not diluted)
1 can (20 oz.) tomatoes
4 cups water
3 tablespoons chili powder
salt to taste

Brown beef, onion and garlic in a large skillet. Combine with other ingredients in large kettle. Bring to a boil, lower heat, cover and simmer for half an hour.

In even the most casual of kitchen encounters it will be found that a gourmet has been there before. Here is a "quickie" recipe that shows that presence — wine instead of water!

1 pound ground beef
1 cup onion, finely chopped
2 cloves garlic, finely chopped
1½ tablespoons chili powder
1 can (16 oz.) tomatoes

2 teaspoons salt
2 teaspoons oregano
1 teaspoon basil
½ cup red wine
2 cans (16 oz.) kidney beans, drained

Brown beef, onion and garlic. Drain off fat. In a large pot combine all ingredients and simmer covered for thirty minutes. If made the day before, add one-fourth cup more of wine fifteen minutes before serving.

This Chili Con Carne can be made on some idle Sunday, refrigerated and served two days later. In fact, it is better two days old than when first taken off the stove, principally because the bay leaves remain breathing through the mixture.

2 pounds chuck beef, coarsely ground
¼ cup olive oil
1 quart water
1 green pepper, diced
2 onions, diced
2 cloves garlic, chopped

2 bay leaves
2 packages chili seasoning
1½ tablespoons sugar
¼ teaspoon ground cumin
1 tablespoon salt
chili peppers to taste

Sear meat and olive oil over hot heat, stirring occasionally until red of meat disappears. Add about one quart of water, pepper, onions, garlic and bay leaves. Cook covered at a bubbling simmer for one hour. Add the rest of the ingredients and simmer for thirty minutes. Add small amount of cornmeal or flour if thickening is desired. Refrigerate forty-eight hours before removing bay leaves and serving.

HOME LATE (Serves 8)

This one comes almost entirely pre-mixed or from a can, and is probably the most "beany" recipe in the book.

1 large onion, chopped
1 can (20 oz.) peeled tomatoes
2½ pounds ground beef
3 cans (15 oz.) chili style brown beans
1 can (15 oz.) kidney beans, drained
1 package chili seasoning
2 teaspoons chili powder

Simmer onion and tomatoes together in a large pot for twenty minutes. Brown beef, drain off grease, and add with rest of ingredients to onions and tomatoes. Bring to a boil and simmer for thirty minutes. Add water if necessary.

Here is another refrigerated Chili Con Carne that has lots more flavor after a day standing in the chill. A word of caution: when purchasing canned chili beans, make sure they are beans in gravy for the correct taste.

1 large onion, minced
2 tablespoons bacon fat
1½ pounds ground round steak
1 tablespoon sugar
1½ teaspoons salt

fresh ground black pepper to taste
dash of cayenne pepper
1 can (20 oz.) tomatoes
½ package or 1¾ ounces chili seasoning
3 cans (15 oz.) chili beans

Sauté onion in two tablespoons of bacon fat in a large pan until soft. Add meat and cook until it has lost its red color. Add sugar, salt, pepper and tomatoes. Cover and cook for twenty minutes. Add chili seasoning and cook five minutes more. Then add the chili beans and cook an additional ten minutes. Add water as desired. Let stand for one day in refrigerator, then reheat.

(Serves 6)

This is deceptive. It is so easy to make you won't believe it, while tasting like a Chili Con Carne that has cooked all day.

2 onions, sliced

2 tablespoons butter

2 pounds ground beef

1½ teaspoons salt

½ teaspoon black pepper

1 teaspoon chili powder

2 chili peppers, crushed

1 can (16 oz.) tomatoes

1 can (6 oz.) tomato paste

1 teaspoon sugar

1 can (4 oz.) mushrooms, drained

1 can (16 oz.) kidney beans, drained

Cook onions in butter until soft. Add beef and brown. Add salt, black pepper, chili powder and crushed chili peppers, tomatoes, tomato paste and sugar and cook one hour over low heat. Add mushrooms and kidney beans and simmer fifteen minutes longer.

What will it be, Chili Con Carne or spaghetti sauce? Here is a recipe that allows you to change your mind midway. You may even go further than anybody ever has before and, by adding 1½ cups sour cream when you serve, make a sort of chili borscht.

1½ pounds ground beef
3 small onions, chopped
1 large green pepper, chopped
2 tablespoons oil
1 teaspoon ground black pepper
½ teaspoon ground red pepper
2 teaspoons salt

basil to taste
garlic salt to taste
1 can (10 oz.) stewed tomatoes
1 can (8 oz.) tomato sauce
4 teaspoons chili powder
1 teaspoon paprika
1 can (16 oz.) light red kidney beans, drained
1 can (16 oz.) dark red kidney beans, drained

Brown meat, onions, and green pepper in oil. Season with pepper, salt, basil, and garlic salt. Here you can change your mind and go for spaghetti sauce if you like.

If you insist on chili, add remaining ingredients except kidney beans. Cook until the peppers are tender. Add beans, heat and serve.

HURRY UP! *(Serves 6)*

Finally, a sweet touch with the use of Spanish onions, large bulbed, and mild flavored. Originally the name "Spanish onion" was applied only to imported stock, but now it is used more broadly. So make sure you get what you ask for.

2 large Spanish onions, diced
2 tablespoons shortening
3 pounds coarse ground beef
1 clove garlic, diced
1 tablespoon black pepper
2 chili peppers, crushed

1 teaspoon ground cumin
1 can (20 oz.) tomatoes
2 cans (6 oz.) tomato paste
2 cups water
4 cans (20 oz.) brown beans in chili sauce

Fry onions in shortening until golden. Add meat and garlic and fry until meat is browned. Add all other ingredients, except beans, and bring to a boil. Cover and simmer one hour. Add beans and simmer for 10 more minutes, then serve.

ODD FELLOW CHILIS

One of the pleasures of compiling *The Chili Cookbook* has been the opportunity it has afforded while roaming over the earth on other duties or pleasure trips, to keep one eye open for recipes containing the basic ingredients of Chili Con Carne — red peppers mixed with meat and whatever national ingenuity could add to that.

Not surprising, the most spectacular discovery was the bond that seems to unite chili lovers all over the world. In Libya, for example, there was Saleh Abbou Abdel Salam, a colonel in Libya's army intelligence, who drove the editors from Bengazi to an oasis in the Tripolitania Desert to taste what he described as the finest chili in the world. Driving through the desert on the way to the oasis, he put it this way:

"I love you both, in my way. I feel a small electrical flash of love go out toward anybody who loves chili the way I do, no matter who he is or where. I immediately become interested in them. I may not show it, my friends, but that is the truth. I wish to guide them, protect them. I am a good Libyan chili eater."

And so he was. Though the Chili Con Carne we found at the oasis certainly was not "the finest in the world," it was unusual and it was good, and is found in this section under the name "El Gheriat esc-Scherghia."

And on it went everywhere. By other names, of course, the dish we know as Chili Con Carne is loved throughout the world. Here, then, you will find some of the most unusual recipes for Chili Con Carne you have ever seen, the only alterations being those ingredients you would have trouble purchasing at the average supermarket.

So, Chili Eaters of the World, now that you have tried the rest why not try what might very well be the best? This chapter is for those with a true spirit of adventure — for those who have tried everything else and still want more. Begin here.

LIVERPOOL *(Serves 4 or 5)*

This one was found in Lancashire County at the Mersey River's edge after a day at Aintree, and what a surprise it was!

½ pound ground mutton
1 tablespoon oil
1 teaspoon salt
1/8 teaspoon red pepper
3 tablespoons chili powder
1 large onion, grated
2 cloves garlic, minced

1 can (16 oz.) tomato paste
1 can (16 oz.) tomato juice
½ pound cheddar cheese
1 cup Parmesan cheese
1 can (6 oz.) black olives, chopped
2 cans (16 oz.) kidney beans, drained

Brown meat in oil, add salt, red pepper, chili powder, onion, garlic, tomato paste and juice and cook until meat is tender. Then add both cheeses, stir in olives and beans and cook slowly about ten minutes until cheese is melted. Let stand one hour until all the flavor is absorbed, reheat and serve.

From a cafe in the old town on Via San Biagio, here is one everybody who likes Italian cookery will enjoy.

1 pound ground beef
1 can (16 oz.) kidney beans, drained
1 large onion, diced
3 tablespoons chili powder
1 can (8 oz.) tomato sauce
2 sauce cans water
1 clove garlic, minced
salt and pepper to taste
½ cup Parmesan cheese, grated

Brown beef, then add all other ingredients except the cheese. Cover and simmer one hour. Turn off heat, add cheese, cover and let stand ten minutes before serving.

ATHENS *(Serves 6 to 8)*

Here is one invented by a Greek friend who owns a cafe near Syntagma Square. Imagine the piquancy of the green tomato!

¼ pound beef suet
6 medium onions, sliced
3 pounds lean beef, cut in cubes
6 green tomatoes, peeled and quartered
2 slices dry bread
2 cloves garlic, split

1 teaspoon Metaxa brandy
1 tablespoon chili powder
1 tablespoon cider or red wine vinegar
1 tablespoon brown sugar
salt to taste
beans, optional (drained)

Chop and melt suet in a heavy frying pan. Sauté onions until golden brown. Remove onions. Sauté beef quickly to seal in juices, then remove from pan. In a large stewing pan mix the rendered suet, onions and tomatoes in boiling water to cover. Add bread thoroughly rubbed with garlic and cook five minutes. Add meat and Metaxa, season with chili powder and cook gently for thirty minutes. Then add vinegar, sugar and salt. Cook for five more minutes and serve over beans of your choice.

EL GHERIAT ESC-SCHERGHIA

Serves 4 or 5)

Here is the one the "good Libyan chili eater" Saleh Abbou Abdel Salam introduced us to. He called it "the finest chili in the world," but then he has never been in the U.S.A.

½ green pepper, diced
1 tablespoon chili powder
1 teaspoon lemon juice
¼ teaspoon salt
½ teaspoon black pepper
1 can (16 oz.) red beans, drained

3 tablespoons onion, diced
1 tablespoon butter
1 pound ground beef
1 can (20 oz.) tomatoes
½ tomato can water
1 small potato, diced

Brown onions in butter, then add beef and brown. Add tomatoes, water, potato, green pepper, chili powder, lemon juice, salt and pepper and cook slowly for one hour. Add beans, simmer half an hour, and serve.

VALENCIA *(Serves 8)*

The discovery of this one is too detailed to go into here. But it was found in a can purchased from a Stockholm grocery shelf, and later traced to Spain where it was made.

1 cup lard
¼ pound ground beef suet
½ cup onions, chopped
5 large cloves garlic, chopped
1 pound ground (lean) beef
1 cup celery, chopped
½ cup raw carrots, grated
2 cans (16 oz.) kidney beans, drained
1 can (8 oz.) tomato sauce

1 can (6 oz.) tomato paste
1 can (16 oz.) tomatoes, sieved
½ cup potatoes, chopped
1 tablespoon salt, or salt to taste
½ teaspoon ground red pepper
½ teaspoon black pepper
½ can chili powder (about 3½ tablespoons)
½ teaspoon brown sugar
1 tablespoon flour
1 cup water

Put lard in large skillet and heat, add ground suet. When suet browns, skim off the browned fat. Add onions and garlic. When they begin to brown add meat, mashing constantly with potato masher until it begins to brown. Add celery, carrots, beans, tomato sauce, tomato paste, also tomatoes and potatoes. Cook briskly for one hour, stirring constantly. Add salt, red and black pepper, chili powder and sugar. Dissolve flour in one cup of water and add gradually to mixture, still stirring. Cook twenty minutes longer and serve.

Not far from the Hotel Continental in downtown Bogotá, near the busy Santander Square, an offbeat Colombian restaurant surprises visitors with this simple little recipe.

2 pounds ground round steak
2 tablespoons butter
1 Bermuda onion, chopped fine
1 green pepper, chopped fine
1 can (20 oz.) tomatoes
1 can (8 oz.) tomato sauce
1 teaspoon sugar
1 teaspoon chili peppers, crushed

1 cup chili sauce
1 bay leaf
beans, optional
According to taste:
Tabasco sauce
liquid hickory smoke
bitters
garlic juice
celery salt

Brown meat in butter, add onion and green pepper and sauté for about ten minutes. Add remaining ingredients, stir all together and simmer for one and one half hours or longer (the longer the better). Just before serving add beans of your choice and heat through.

TORONTO *(Serves 4 or 5)*

Wonderful Toronto! Of course chili would be found there, in a cafe near the intersection of Yonge and Queen Streets, just north of the Union Station.

1½ pounds ground round steak
4 medium onions, chopped
2 tablespoons fat
1 cup chopped celery
2 cups green pepper, chopped
3 tablespoons tomato sauce
2 tablespoons uncooked rice
1 can (16 oz.) kidney or pinto beans, drained
chili powder to taste

Brown beef and onions in two tablespoons of fat. Add remaining ingredients, cover with water and simmer for forty-five minutes.

(Serves 3 or 4) MIAMI BEACH

Here is the fastest-made chili in the book. And it is not from a restaurant, but was found at a friend's house out by Miami International Airport.

1 pound ground chuck
1 package chili seasoning
½ cup water
1 can (16 oz.) tomatoes
1 can (16 oz.) kidney beans, drained
1 can (8 oz.) chicken gumbo soup

Brown beef in a large skillet, stirring frequently. Stir chili seasoning into meat, add water, tomatoes, kidney beans and soup. Bring to a boil, reduce heat and simmer covered for ten minutes.

KUALA LUMPUR *(Serves 8)*

In hilly country, in a traditional Chinese hash joint in the town's congested center and near the Klang River, we sampled this unusual Chili Con Carne while gazing at the Malaysian architecture through the window.

2 pounds ground beef
2 cups white wine
1 medium sized green pepper, diced
½ cup celery, diced
2 medium sized onions, diced

1 tablespoon chili powder
½ teaspoon chili pepper, crushed
½ cup water chestnuts, cut up
½ pound pea pods
2 cans (16 oz.) beans (of choice), drained

Brown meat in half a cup of white wine. Add green peppers, celery and onions and cook until fully sautéed. Add chili powder and chili pepper and remaining wine. Cook for two hours over low heat, adding water chestnuts and pea pods about 10 minutes before serving with the beans.

Via a Delhi Transport Service bus southward from the Ashoka Hotel, somewhere in that teeming city (so easy to get lost in) browsing in cafes turned up this one.

½ cup barley
1 pound ground lamb
1 large onion, chopped
6 stalks celery, chopped
1 can (32 oz.) peeled tomatoes
¼ teaspoon curry powder

2 tablespoons red wine
1 can (16 oz.) kidney beans, drained
2 chili peppers, chopped
pinch of brown sugar
salt and pepper to taste

Cook barley in water to cover for forty-five minutes. Set aside. Brown meat, onion and celery until onion and celery are soft. Add remaining ingredients and cooked barley, and simmer for one-half-hour.

BUENOS AIRES *(Serves 4 or 5)*

Beef is the thing in Argentina, and it is really good. And here is a Chili Con Carne that is heavy on the beef proportionately, sampled in a cafe on the Calle Florida with its expensive shops and a mall closed to traffic every evening.

1½ pounds ground (lean) beef
2 Medium onions, chopped
1 cup celery, chopped
2 cans (16 oz.) kidney beans, drained
3 cans (8 oz.) tomato juice
2 tablespoons sugar
3 teaspoons chili powder

Brown meat in skillet, stirring constantly, because there is no fat used. Add onions and celery while meat is browning. Then add one can of kidney beans. Mash the second can of beans to a soft pulp, using a fork, mashing a few beans at a time (a blender works better, using a little of the tomato juice if extra liquid is required). Add mashed beans to meat mixture. Follow with tomato juice, sugar and chili powder. Cover and simmer for thirty minutes, stirring occasionally, and serve.

Think Chili Con Carne is American only? Think again! They are very proud of this one on congested Allenby Road, especially after an evening at the Mograbi Theater.

1 bunch green onions (including two inches of the green tops)
1 can (8 oz.) tomato soup
1 soup can water
1 pound corned beef, broken into small pieces
1 can (16 oz.) kidney beans, drained
1 tablespoon chili powder
2 chili peppers, cut into small pieces
salt to taste
pepper to taste

Cook green onions and tops (cut up), tomato soup and water together for about five minutes over simmering heat. Add corned beef, kidney beans, chili powder and peppers and cook over moderate heat for about ten to twelve minutes. Salt and pepper to taste and serve.

BERLIN *(Serves 8 to 12)*

Herr and Frau Wirtschaftswunder add their own magic touch to the universal potage at their charming little cafe near Ernst Reuterplatz. The recipe was rather hard to pull out of them, but here it is.

2 pounds dried pinto beans
3 cans (6 oz.) tomato paste
4 pounds ground (lean) chuck
2 teaspoons salt
¼ teaspoon black pepper
4 tablespoons chili powder
8 tablespoons olive oil

2 large onions, chopped
½ green pepper, chopped
2 cloves garlic, chopped
2 tablespoons dry mustard, heaping
1 cup beer
1 cup sugar

Soak beans in cold water overnight, removing bad beans that float to top. Then cook beans in same water until tender. Stir in tomato paste. Combine beef, salt, pepper and chili powder in skillet with four tablespoons of olive oil and cook until meat is brown.

In another skillet combine onions, green pepper, garlic and remaining olive oil and cook until onions are golden brown. Pour all ingredients except sugar, mustard and beer into beans, stirring gently. Blend mustard and beer and add to mixture. Cover and cook over low heat for fifteen to twenty minutes, adding sugar in the last five minutes. Serve in soup bowls with a stein of beer on the side.

During a parade for the Virgin of Sapopan, patroness of the city, we sat in a cafe near the Teatro Degollado and enjoyed this one.

1 pound ground beef
½ cup onions, finely chopped
½ cup celery, finely chopped
½ cup green peppers, finely chopped
2 tablespoons fat
1 clove garlic, chopped
½ teaspoon sugar

4 cans (8 oz.) tomato sauce
2 cans (16 oz.) brown beans
1 square unsweetened chocolate
2 teaspoons chili powder
1 teaspoon salt
2 tablespoons cornmeal

Cook beef, onion, celery and green pepper in two tablespoons of fat. When meat has lost its color and onion has become transparent, add remaining ingredients except cornmeal. Simmer, stirring occasionally, for forty-five minutes to one hour. Add cornmeal about ten minutes before serving.

COPENHAGEN *(Serves 6 to 8)*

There is a small place just off Hans Christian Andersen Boulevard where, in Royal Copenhagen porcelain bowls and with Georg Jensen spoons, this mild but delicious chili is served. The owner, Lars Hansen, said the recipe is the result of continual experimentation, or "toning down," since his country-men shy from the too-hot variety of Chili Con Carne.

3 pounds ground chuck
2 tablespoons oil
salt and pepper to taste
3 large onions, chopped
1 stalk celery, chopped

3 cans (8 oz.) tomato soup
½ bottle catsup
2 cans (16 oz.) kidney beans, drained
1 quart water
½ cup aquavit

Brown meat in skillet with oil, salt and pepper. Remove meat and put into large kettle. Add a bit more oil to meat juices in skillet, then add onions and celery, simmering slowly until both are tender. Combine tomato soup, catsup, beans and water with meat in kettle and put on stove over a low flame. Simmer for forty-five minutes. During the last fifteen minutes add the aquavit, then serve and eat hearty, mild chili lovers!

NAGASAKI

There still are some crooked streets and tiered houses enclosing the beautiful deep-cut bay in this tragic city. On one of those streets, at a friend's house, this gentle chicken Chili Con Carne was found.

1½-inch slice dry bread
2 tablespoons seedless raisins
¼ square bitter chocolate
2 tablespoons toasted almonds
3 tablespoons olive oil
1 tablespoon onion, minced
1 small clove garlic, peeled and minced
2 tablespoons flour
dash of ground cloves

¼ teaspoon ground cinnamon
1 tablespoon chili powder
1 can (4 oz.) tomato sauce
1 cup boiling chicken stock
1 large chicken, boiled
½ teaspoon salt
1 can (16 oz.) kidney beans, drained
1 tablespoon grated cheddar cheese
2 tablespoons sake (Japanese wine)
cooked rice

Put bread, raisins, chocolate and almonds through a food chopper together. Heat oil, add onions and minced garlic. Stir in flour, cloves, cinnamon, chili powder, tomato sauce and chicken stock, stirring constantly over low heat until the mixture thickens and boils.

Add chicken pieces, salt, drained beans and sake.

Place in casserole, sprinkle with grated cheese and put into oven (375 degrees) for about thirty minutes. Serve with the traditional bowl of rice on the side.

KATMANDU *(Serves 6 to 8)*

There was the Festival of the Cow when we were there, with Nepalese children marching through the streets calling out the names of their deceased relatives. We sat enjoying this chili in a red brick house four stories high — the Himalayas in the distance. Afterwards, a strong Nepal cigarette.

2 pounds dry pinto beans, soaked overnight
¼ cup cornmeal
3 pounds ground beef
pinto of water

4 cloves garlic, mashed with salt added
½ cup chili powder
¼ teaspoon oregano
2 chili peppers, crushed

Cook pre-soaked pinto beans until tender, about one hour, and add cornmeal, simmering for fifteen minutes. Brown meat and put into a kettle with the water. Add mashed garlic, chili powder, oregano and boil for forty-five minutes. When serving, put a portion of beans in a bowl, then a portion of meat, and sprinkle with crushed chili pepper.

HEIDELBERG

This was discovered on the Friedrich-Ebert Anlage, near the garden and the station. The view of wooded hills and the misty rose-red ruin of the castle was dreamy, all right, but we managed to get the recipe before we left.

5 strips bacon	1 can (16 oz.) kidney beans, drained
1 pound ground beef	1 can (6 oz.) tomato sauce
salt and pepper to taste	1 can (12 oz.) beer
1 large onion, diced	2 beer cans water
1 green pepper, diced	1 tablespoon chili powder
5 ribs of celery, diced	

Brown bacon and dice it. Brown beef with salt and pepper. Add to bacon the onion, pepper and celery and cook until onion is golden brown.

In a kettle combine kidney beans, tomato sauce, beer and water and heat. Add chili powder and cook slowly for about one hour, keeping covered.

CAPE TOWN (Serves 6 to 8)

There will always be an England, even in South Africa! Note the touches that make this one purely Anglo-Saxon — for example, currant jelly and scallops!

3½ pounds ground beef
1 large onion, sliced
1 dozen scallops
1 teaspoon garlic salt
4 tablespoons chili powder

salt and pepper to taste
1 can (8 oz.) tomato sauce
1 tablespoon currant jelly
3 cups water
2 cans (16 oz.) kidney beans, drained

Fry meat, onion and scallops until beef is gray. Drain off fat. Transfer to kettle and add all other ingredients except beans. Cover, bring to a boil, then lower heat and simmer for an hour-and-a-half. Add beans half an hour before serving.

INDEX

Index by name of recipe

A

A Bed of Beans 46
A Bit of Mexico 33
Accent on Peppercorns 64
Adventuring 73
A la Spaghetti 108
Allegheny Highway 97
Amarillo 18
Athens 132
Azteca 104

B

Berlin 142

Blanco's Rio Grande 45
Bogotá 135
Bouillon and Mushrooms 100
Breathe Easy 78
Brown Derby, The 40
Buenos Aires 140
By Any Other Name 109

C

Cannonadeer 52
Cape Town 148
Chasen's Famous Chili 51
Cinnamon Flavored 99
Cocoa Flavored 103

Communal 76
Copenhagen 144

D

Dad's Favorite 43
Dallas County Jailhouse Chili 17
Dash of Curry 110
Deep Breather 41
Dexterous 119

E

Easy Does It 114
El Gheriat esc-Scherghia 133

Even Stephen 56

F

Far West 69
Few Rules 116
Fire Call 84
For Millionaires Only 68

G

Green Pepper 74
Guadalajara 143

H

Heat It Up 121
Heidelberg 147
Hell's Fire 89
Home Late 122
Hot Pants Style 38
Hot Porker 88
Houston's Best 19
Hurry Up! 126

I

Inferno 92
Iowa Red 107

It's Pickled 71
It's the Dickens 32

J

Jalapeño Authentico 35

K

Katmandu 146
Kid's Delight 42
Kuala Lumpur 138

L

Lady Bird Johnson's
  Pedernales River Special 29
Leisure Time 117
Let It Stand 44
Liverpool 130

M

Masa Masa 28
Miami Beach 137
Midwest Cayenne 65
Minnesota Style 77
Mushroom Sniffle 66

N

Nagasaki 145
Naples 131
New Delhi 139
No Effort, 120
No Exit 85
No Retreat 90
No Strain 113
No Tomatoes, Please 98

O

Off the Farm 101
Old Carney 53

Onions and Stuff 50
On the Patio 102
On the Run 124

P

Pancho Villa 30
Pinto Beans 49
Porky 72
Presto! 125

R

Rapido 37
Ring-Around 118

S

San Antonio 20
Scorcher 86
Shades of Texas 39
Sirloin and Rice 96
Slightly Smashed 55
Sly One, The 54
Spontaneous 115
S.S. Johnnie, The 70
Standby 123
Stomach Warmer 36
Sweet Suet 31

T

Taps 60
Tear-Jerker 67
Tel Aviv 141
Three-Hour Beans 57
Thick and Sassy 34
Togetherness 58
Toronto 136
Truck Stop 105

W

Waterfront 75
Wheeler-Dealer 106
When Autumn Comes 91

V

Valencia 134
Vegetarian Dreamboat 59
Volcano 87

Index by outstanding ingredients or methods of preparation

A

Almonds 145
Aquavit 144

B

Bacon 88, 117, 147
Bacon drippings 75, 77, 101
Baked 56
Barley 139
Bay leaf 34, 58, 72, 101, 104, 121
Bean liquid, simmered 65, 109
Beans, as a bed 46

Beans, brown chili-style 122
Beans, dried, preparation of 49
Beans, meat cooked together with 58
Beef broth 105
Beef heart 36
Beef stock 50, 57
Beer 142
Bitters 135
Black pepper 78
Blender used to blend vegetables 69, 89
Boiled, chowder-style 60;
  with beans 99;
  with stew beef chunks 104
Boiled recipes 33, 39, 42
Bouillon cubes, beef 100

Bread, dried 132
Butter 51

C

Carrots 134
Casserole 37
Catsup 70, 144
Cayenne pepper 65, 88
Celery 67, 110, 136
Celery seed 110
Chicken 145
Chicken fat 20
Chicken gumbo soup 137

Chili beef soup 113
Chili powder 84, 85, 120, 146
Chili sauce 70, 73
Chili seasoning 19, 114, 121, 122
Chocolate 143
Cinnamon 99
Cocoa 103
Corned beef 141
Cumin seed 17, 33, 34, 57, 69, 91
Currant jelly 148
Curry powder 110, 139

F

Flour, kneaded in beef 103

G

Garlic   20, 32, 34, 38, 41, 78, 86
Goose grease   35
Green onions   115
Green peppers   74, 136
Ground vegetables   69

H

Ham   37
Hickory smoke, liquid   135
Horseradish, dry   45

L

Lamb, ground   139
Lard   134

M

Macaroni   92
Macaroni shells   119
Meatballs   45
Meatless   59
Metaxa brandy   132
Mexican maize   28

Mushrooms 66, 96, 100
Mustard, dry 85, 142
Mutton, ground 130

O

Olive oil 53
Olives, ripe 96, 101, 102
Onionless 32, 33
Onion soup 115
Onions 50, 67
Onions, sliced 124
Onions, Spanish 126
Oregano 33, 52, 57

P

Paprika 106
Parmesan cheese 85, 131
Pea pods 138
Peppercorns 64
Pepper pods, black and red 30
Pepper, sweet 17
Peppers, green 19, 51, 74
Peppers, jalapeño and melrose 35
Pickling spices 71
Pinto beans, basic recipe 49
Pinto beans, bulk of recipe 51, 57, 89
Pinto beans, specified use of 35, 39

Pinto beans, three-hour preparation 57
Pork 37, 50, 51, 52, 53, 72, 87
Pork sausage 85
Pork shoulder, cubed 101
Potatoes 133, 134

Raisins 145
Rice 96

S

Sage 92
Sake 145
Scallops 148
Spaghetti 108
Spaghetti ring 118
Spaghetti sauce, chili used as 125
Steak sirloin 96, 109
Steak, ground round 135
Steak, top round 68, 108
Suet, beef 17, 31, 40, 45, 46, 90
Sugar 142

Tomato 55
Tomato juice 19, 88, 140
Tomato sauce 64, 77
Tomato soup 20, 67, 85, 107, 118, 119
Turmeric 45

V

Veal 117
Vegetarian 59
Vinegar 43, 73

W

Water chestnuts 138
Wine, white 138

OTHER BEST-SELLING P/S/S COOKBOOKS ARE:

THE COFFEE COOKBOOK

THE RUM COOKBOOK

THE HENRI CHARPENTIER COOKBOOK

THE CELEBRITY COOKBOOK

COOKING FOR ORGIES AND OTHER LARGE PARTIES

THE BACK TO COOKING COOKBOOK

12 GREAT PARTIES

THE GOLFERS' COOKBOOK

THE PICASSO & PIE BUFFET COOKBOOK

CHOCOLATE KICKS AND OTHER RECIPES FOR THE CHOCOLATE ADDICT

If not available at your bookseller's, they may
be ordered directly from the publisher.
For complete list, write:

o

Dept. CH-4

PRICE / STERN / SLOAN
Publishers, Inc.
410 North La Cienega Boulevard
Los Angeles, California 90048